Simp
Mac

A complete guide to Mac OS X

Richard Hill

published by **MacUnlimited** London
www.macunlimited.com

Published by **MacUnlimited**
19 Nassau Street, London W1W 7AF
www.macunlimited.com

Printed and bound in the UK by Clays Limited, St Ives plc

ISBN 1-904223-00-1

This is the first in a series of books from MacUnlimited
designed to help you get more from your Mac. You'll find
updates, corrections and discussion online at
www.macunlimited.com

www.macunlimited.net
Mac-dedicated Internet service provider
dialup hosting co-location streaming

www.macunlimited.com
the online Mac magazine
news reviews features tutorials

Contents

About the author

Richard Hill is a writer and journalist specialising in computing and technology, and is a long-standing Macintosh fan. He's been using Macs since 1988. Richard was also Deputy Editor on the UK Macintosh magazine *MacFormat*, and went on to edit *Mobile Computer User* and *WAP* magazines.

Acknowledgements

Project editor: Alex Summersby
Cover and book design: tablet.co.uk
Cover photography by Sebastian Smith
Special thanks to the Tech Support team at macunlimited.net for their generous advice.

Foreword

Karen Harvey
Editor of MacUser

There's no doubt that Mac OS X is the biggest thing to happen in the Mac market since the introduction of the first Mac in 1984.

Despite having by far the best and most easy-to-use interface in the world, the Mac has been the butt of many a geeky joke from the Windows world for its lack of buzzword-compliant features such as pre-emptive multi-tasking. Apple has long been striving to radically revamp the Mac OS to bring it into line with such buzzwords, but it took until Steve Jobs's re-emergence as Apple CEO for it to get done. And there's no doubt that Apple has done a fantastic job with Mac OS X, which can not only run old Mac applications, but gives developers ways to update their applications quickly to take advantage of the new OS.

For users, the changes in the interface will be the most dramatic. The familiar Mac interface has been usurped by the truly beautiful Aqua, which looks and feels like something new, elegant, and truly exciting. Many of the old Mac stalwarts, such as control panels and extensions, are gone too.

And, of course, underneath the glitz of the interface, there's the power of a Unix system, with all the operating system muscle that this entails. Unix is one of the world's most powerful and stable operating systems, and a firm favourite – but has never been known for its usability or friendliness.

That's where Apple comes in. It's no exaggeration to say that Mac OS X is the easiest version of Unix to use, with the most well-designed and genuinely playful interface around. But while it's certainly an easy operating system to use, if you're not familiar with it you can get a little lost. And if you want to get the most out of the new OS, you need something to guide you through it.

That's where this book comes in. One of the things that every Mac user needs is a step-by-step guide to the new OS that goes into the details of how it works and how it differs from the old style Mac. You'll find here all the information you need to work with Mac OS X, whether you're transitioning from an older version or are a complete novice with the Mac.

In this book, Richard Hill takes you from the basics, all the way through to deep into the heart of Mac OS X – and all in a style that's easy to read and understand. By the end of the book, you'll be able to do everything you can do with your current OS, and much more besides.

The book that you have in your hands is an essential guide to Mac OS X. So now, sit down, fire up your Mac with its brand new OS, and start to enjoy it.

Karen Harvey
Editor, MacUser
www.macuser.co.uk

Preface

This book is the first in a series of guides proudly
brought to you by MacUnlimited, the UK's premier
Mac dedicated service provider. We're publishing
these books as a natural extension of our
commitment to serving the Mac community. As a
Mac specialist ISP, MacUnlimited is renowned for
its tech support, and we've taken the same user-
friendly approach in this book. As publishers of
MacUnlimited.com, the online Mac magazine, our
goal is to inform, to guide, and to help you get more
from your Mac... and again, this same philosophy
is behind this complete guide to Mac OS X.

Apple's "next-generation" operating system is a
radical new departure for the Mac, and in that sense
all of us, experienced Mac users as well as complete
computing newcomers, are novices when it comes
to Mac OS X. For that reason we've chosen to start
at the basics in this book and work through Mac OS
X step-by-step. However, we've included special
notes to alert you wherever OS X does things in a
way that might confuse you if you're used to
Microsoft Windows or to previous versions of the
Mac OS. Even so, we've tried to avoid technical
complexities, and we don't believe you need to
know about the guts of OS X – Darwin and Aqua

and Carbon and all that stuff – to get to grips with it. For this reason, we've left that sort of detail to the end of this book.

What this book covers

Each version of the Mac OS to be released receives its own version number. As this edition of *Simply Mac OS X* goes to press, the current version is Mac OS X 10.1, and this book is written with that version in mind. If you have a version of Mac OS X older than 10.1, we urge you to update to get the most out of the book... and to get the most out of your Mac!

Feedback

This is the first book in MacUnlimited's *Simply* series. We'd love to hear what you think of it and what subjects you think we should cover in future books in the series. You can e-mail the editor at **editor@macunlimited.com**, or the author at **richardhill@macunlimited.com**. Please understand that we can't reply to messages personally or offer any technical support beyond the contents of the book itself, although we will read and consider every message we receive.

Updates and corrections

The world of computing changes fast, and new information is always coming to light. Bugs may be found, or updates released at any time. We can't publish a new edition of this book every time, but we can help you keep up to date: we'll publish updates and corrections in our online magazine, which you'll find at **www.MacUnlimited.com**. There's no charge to access it (apart from any normal Internet access costs you pay), and it's available to you at any time. It also brings you a whole range of news, features and articles – check it out!

Introduction

What's the critical element that makes a computer such an important tool? Some say it's the processor, the engine that gives the computer its raw speed. Others swear by the most polished "applications" – the software programs that enable you to perform specific tasks. But while each of these is important, you should never underestimate the role of the operating system that enables the processor and your applications to work together.

Maybe it's the geeky label, but some people have trouble pinning down what an operating system actually does. For many, it's the interface that counts – the combination of menus, icons and other visual components that places a computer in your command. Equally crucial, though, is what lies underneath. The heart of an operating system is its ability to juggle different tasks and continue to function as smoothly and robustly as possible, no matter what you ask of it.

It was this second requirement that was causing Apple Computer, the maker of the world-famous Macintosh computer line, some concern several years ago. The Mac OS, the operating system inside every Macintosh, had won plaudits and millions of devoted users since its introduction in 1984, but users and their applications were starting to ask for more advanced features than it was able to deliver. Apple decided it was time for a new generation of operating system, one that could cope with the demands of computer users today and tomorrow.

Years in the making, Mac OS X is the result, the operating system to take the Mac into the future. To create it, Apple has assembled a coherent suite of tools from scratch rather than following the usual practice of adapting and tweaking what it already had. Mac OS X is based on Unix, a tried-and-tested operating system widely regarded as the most robust operating system available but not noted for its accessibility to non-experts. Apple's taken up the challenge to make a version of Unix that anyone can enjoy using, applying the company's experience in designing friendly interfaces.

The Mac OS has long had a reputation for being one of the easiest operating systems to learn, and to use on a day-to-day basis. Many would contend that it has no equal, and it's certainly had a significant influence on alternatives like Microsoft Windows. Mac OS X has achieved the feat of combining the power of Unix with the simplicity of the Mac OS.

Learning Mac OS X
Mac OS X is at once beautifully simple and compellingly complex. You can grasp its basics and start using it productively within minutes – but it also has a staggering depth of features and tools, which can take far longer to learn. This book will help you get to grips with everything Mac OS X has to offer. We'll help you grasp the underlying logic of Mac OS X, to help you think your own way around the OS and deduce how to complete a task, based on your knowledge of OS X's typical behaviour.

Mac OS X could be the most powerful operating system on the planet; we'll help you become a power user.

I Computer Basics

Beginners start here, as we find out how computers work and what makes the Mac, with Mac OS X, the best option around.

1 A Journey Inside Your Computer

In this chapter, we'll introduce you to basic concepts defining every computer, including a Mac running Mac OS X. This chapter is designed for anyone who has never, or only rarely, used a computer before. You can skip to the next chapter on page 21 if you're familiar with any type of modern computer, such as a Mac or a PC running Microsoft Windows.

What computers are for

Strip away the technology and all that jargon, and what you're left with is a computer's core purpose: to handle information. A computer reads, interprets, analyses, sorts, changes, erases or, with your help, adds to information faster than the most nimble pair of hands on the planet. Every modern computer is designed to the same broad template, with the main components working together in the same way regardless of scale or speed. The **processor** is the heart of every computer. Every piece of information you work with goes through this sliver of electronics. The computer's **memory** is a workspace that holds all the information the processor needs at any given moment.

Quick tip

Computers and other electronic devices are classed as **hardware**. The programs they use, and the files they produce, are classed as **software**.

The contents of the computer's memory change constantly and are pulled from a physical reservoir of information, the **hard disk**. This resides permanently within your computer and is always available to read information from or write new information onto.

These components are supported by many others inside the computer, but these are the three that do the real work. For the processor, memory and hard disk to work together, though, each has to be able to understand the information it receives from the others – they all have to speak the same language, basically... or at least have a very good go-between.

The operating system

This is where the **operating system** or OS comes in. It provides guidelines for the computer to follow, so it's able to understand the information it receives. The operating system has to be written to work with a specific type of processor, which is why only Macintosh computers are able to run the Mac OS.

An operating system is composed in a language or code that the processor can understand, but which is very difficult for people to learn. Mere mortals need an interpreter, which is why every OS has a **user interface**. This translates hard-to-swallow operating system language into a form we can understand, displaying text and images on a screen and enabling us to give the OS instructions.

Today's most advanced user interfaces present information in a rich visual form, with symbols or **icons** representing the files that the operating system uses, as well the storage media holding those files. Mac OS X is one such operating system and interface; alternatives like Microsoft Windows present a different interface.

Quick tip

The formal name for computer memory is RAM or Random Access Memory. It's measured in megabytes (abbreviated MB) or, more and more commonly these days, gigabytes (GB). 1GB equals 1,024MB. The smallest unit you're likely to come across is the kilobyte (abbreviated just K): 1MB equals 1,024K. Surprisingly, the computer's "memory" is not where it stores information – that's the hard disk, the capacity of which is also measured in MB (or GB). This seems confusing, until you realise that the computer is continually swapping information from one to the other – from the hard disk to RAM in order to do something with it, and back from RAM to hard disk when you save it again.

Applications

The operating system alone cannot cater for the demands we make of a computer – there are too many different tasks we want to do. So the OS uses **applications** or programs to provide extra facilities for us to use when we need them. Each application is made with a specific role in mind: it might be designed to work with text, music or photos, for example. An application takes the information it's working with from a **document**, a computer file you might loosely equate with a sheet of paper. The application enables you to change the document, adding or removing information; each application offers its own tools to make this possible.

To make full use of your computer, then, you have to be familiar not only with the operating system's user interface but also with the applications that enable you to complete the tasks you have in mind, whether it's writing a note, designing a picture or playing a game. To make that job easier for you, most applications work within the interface design

All modern computers are made from the same basic components – but, as Apple's iBook proves, it's how you blend the ingredients that counts. Photo courtesy of Apple.

the OS has established, so once you've learned how the interface behaves, you'll understand how most applications will behave as well.

Beyond your computer

It's important for today's computers to be able to swap information, and there are several ways of doing this. The most obvious is to transfer a file onto a **storage medium** that you can insert into another machine. This might be a Zip disk or a CD-ROM, for example.

A more sophisticated method is to link computers directly together, so they can pass information between them. A group of computers connected together is called a **network**. You might find networks in offices or colleges, although small networks are becoming part of many homes too as we buy more computers and want them to talk to one another. Most networks link machines together through cables, although there is an increasing number of wireless networks that rely on radio waves. Mac OS X includes tools to help your Mac connect to and communicate with other machines in a network, both through cables and wirelessly.

Most networks are restricted to a limited group of people, such as the employees of a company. These are known as local networks (or Local Area Networks, hence LANs). But there's one network spanning the world, which anyone can join – the **Internet** or Net. Through the Net, computers around the world can connect with each other to exchange information. The Internet enables you to send and receive messages through **e-mail** or to look up pages of information through the **World Wide Web**, often called simply the Web. You can also transfer files from one computer on the Net to your own, a process called **downloading**. (The reverse process, transferring files from your computer to another on the Net, is logically enough called **uploading**.)

Mac OS X includes a suite of tools to help you connect to the Internet. You can connect to the Net through your office or college network, or through your phone line at home. Internet access at home requires the help of an Internet service provider, a firm that acts as the "bridge" between your computer and the Net.

2 Meet the Mac

Now that we've looked at the basics of computers, this chapter explains what makes a Mac different and shows you the shape of today's Mac OS lineup. If you're already familiar with Macs, you can skip this chapter and the next and go straight to the chapter about installing Mac OS X on page 33.

Thinking different

The relationship between the processor and the operating system is at the heart of a computer. In the late 1970s and early 1980s, when computers first became affordable and accessible enough for individuals to buy them, there were many different varieties or **platforms**, each offering its own distinct combination of processor, operating system and interface. Models of the time included the Apple II, the Commodore Pet and the Sinclair ZX Spectrum. This maze of alternatives simplified during the 1980s as some platforms and manufacturers gained market share and others fell by the wayside. By the end of the decade there were far fewer platforms, each with more users but with limited abilities to exchange information with users of other platforms.

1984 saw the introduction of an innovative, ground-breaking computer platform: the Macintosh. The Mac was different from almost everything that had come before it, offering a graphical interface in an affordable machine. The operating system powering the Mac didn't have a formal name at first – for a long time it was referred to simply as "The System" – but eventually it came to be called the Mac OS.

Counting to X

Today's Macs obviously don't use the same Mac OS as the first Macintosh. As operating systems evolve (with the addition of new features and support for new hardware), new versions are released from time to time. The version numbers step up in whole numbers for major revisions (such as System 7 in 1991 and Mac OS 8 in late 1997) or in point-somethings for incremental upgrades (like Mac OS 7.6, the first to adopt the official "Mac OS" title, in early 1997).

When Mac OS X was released, the traditional Mac OS had reached version 9.1, and this version is still installed on many Macs. Indeed, most Mac OS X users should also install Mac OS 9.1 or 9.2, which

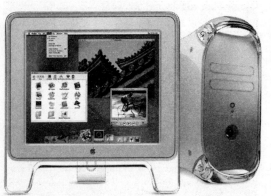

The PowerMac G4 is the flagship of the Mac range. Aimed largely at designers, it's one of the fastest and most versatile computers you can buy. Photo courtesy of Apple.

is included on a separate CD-ROM in the Mac OS X package, so they can keep using the older Mac applications they already own.

There are three parallel versions of the Mac OS at present:

Mac OS 9

Quick tip

To use Mac OS 9 alongside Mac OS X, you must have at least version 9.1, which contains a tool to make it easy to switch to Mac OS X. See the Guided Tour "Living with the Legacy" on page 201.

Mac OS 9 is the pinnacle of the evolution that began in 1984 with the original Macintosh. It has its own "Platinum" look and its own ways of working, sometimes significantly different from Mac OS X's. (We'll point out some of the most important of these as we go.) It also has thousands of applications available for it, and can run in tandem with OS X so that you can keep using those older applications. The latest version of Mac OS 9 is Mac OS 9.2.1.

Mac OS X

Mac OS X represents a new beginning for the Mac OS, a foundation for new features and capabilities that will take it into the future. (For details of some of these, see page 215.) It incorporates many changes from Mac OS 9, but is able to work alongside that version on the same computer. The latest version is Mac OS X 10.1.

Mac OS X is so powerful and versatile that it's simple to surf the Web, play a movie, blast out a music track and present a photo on-screen – all at the same time.

Mac OS X Server

This is a special edition of Mac OS X, available to buy separately. Mac OS X Server is designed for computers with the specific role of constantly delivering material to other computers, whether that's over a local network or through the Internet. Mac OS X Server includes a vast selection of additional applications to enable any modern Mac to act as a powerful server, and is aimed at companies rather than individuals.

Mac OS X Server is developed separately from Mac OS X itself, and may carry a different version number on occasion. Apple does not guarantee that applications written for Mac OS X will work on Mac OS X Server: it's really designed as a complete, independent solution for a specific task. For this reason, this book is not intended for users of Mac OS X Server.

Quick tip

To find out more about Mac OS X Server, visit **www.apple.com/ macosx/server/**

3 Keys and Controls

Like any operating system, Mac OS X has rules and conventions that it's important to learn. Much of the information below will be familiar if you've used a computer before, but some of it is specific to Macs, and some new to Mac OS X.

Visual elements

Mac OS X presents many different elements on your screen as part of its interface:

Window
A frame containing information, which you can typically move around the screen, resize, and close when you have finished with it.

Dialogue box
A frame requesting information from you, such as locating a file to open or confirming an action you may want to take.

Icon
A symbol or picture on your screen, which can represent a file used by your Mac or a command in an application window.

Menu

A list of options activated by clicking on a text label at the top of the screen.

Pull-down menu

Placed within a window or dialogue box, a pull-down menu appears as one option with up and down arrows next to it. Click on the menu and hold down the mouse button, and you'll see further options listed.

Button

A particular kind of symbol or graphic on screen, which you click on to activate a process or action you want to take.

Checkbox

A box next to an option within a window or dialogue box. Click in the box to add a tick to select that option, or click again to remove the tick to disable the option.

Radio button

A special kind of checkbox, round in shape rather than square. Radio buttons are used when you can choose only one of a range of options. Click in one to select it, and all others are de-selected.

Tab

You can get a row of tabs within a window or dialogue box, like the A to Z cards you might use to separate files in the office. Clicking on the appropriate tab reveals new information or options. (Don't confuse this kind of on-screen tab with the Tab *key*...)

Field

An enclosed area within a window or dialogue box, inviting you to enter a specific piece of information – like filling in a form. Click in the appropriate field and you'll see a cursor so you can start typing.

Folders and paths

Throughout this book, we'll guide you to a particular folder. Some folders are "nested" inside others, so you'll have to open the outer folder to find the one you need, essentially following a "path". Folder paths are written in bold using the format **Applications/Utilities**, which means open the Applications folder on your hard disk, then the Utilities folder you see inside.

Some folder paths begin with ~: this means the path starts at your own Home folder, which will carry the name you gave it. So **~/Documents** means open the Documents folder in your Home.

Menu commands

We'll be offering instructions and tips for using Mac OS X where we'll mention a particular menu command to select. Menu commands are written in bold using the format **File > Open**, which means: go to the File menu and select the Open command. The Apple menu is the menu in the top left of the screen with the Apple Computer logo.

Know your keyboard

Some of the tips we give involve keyboard shortcuts, where you can hit a key combination rather than selecting the command from a menu. This involves holding down one or more keys – known as modifier keys – while you press a further key. The modifier keys on your keyboard are:

⇧ **Shift**

On your keyboard, this key may be marked with an arrow pointing upwards. It's used to capitalise letters or select some punctuation characters as well as acting as a modifier key.

⌘ **Command**
This key is typically labelled with the Apple logo or a symbol like a four-leaf clover.

⌥ **Option**
On your keyboard, this key may be labelled "**Alt**" or may show a symbol suggestive of branching off from a line.

ctrl **Control**
This key may be labelled "**Crtl**" on your keyboard.

Keyboard shortcuts are written using the format **Command-Q**, which means hold down the Command key and press Q. (This is the command for quitting an application.)

Windows users

The Mac OS uses the Command key as the main modifier key where Microsoft Windows tends to use the Control key.

Keys of note

There are a few other keys mentioned in the book:

⇥ **Tab**
This key adds an indent at the beginning of a paragraph. It's on the far left of the keyboard and may show an arrow pointing right and touching a vertical line.

← **Delete**
This key, sometimes misnamed the "backspace" key, erases the character you've just typed. It's at the right of the top row of alphabet keys on your keyboard, and may show an arrow pointing to the left. On extended keyboards, it's important not to confuse this with the key sometimes marked "**Del**" or showing a right-pointing arrow with a cross in it ⌦, which erases the character to the *right* of your cursor.

⏎ **Return**
This key is under Delete on the right of the alphabet
keys on the keyboard, and may show an arrow that
turns clockwise and ends pointing to the left.

Using your mouse

To use Mac OS X effectively, you should get used
to the various ways you can select and manipulate
objects on the screen with your mouse (or your
trackpad if you're using a PowerBook or iBook).
The basic principle is that the pointer on screen
moves as you move your mouse around (or as you
move your finger on the trackpad). To do things on
your Mac, you move the pointer to icons or menu
items on screen, then perform various actions:

Click
A single firm press and release of your mouse
button (make sure you don't move the mouse while
you do this). A click is typically used to select icons
or menus. You will see the object that the pointer is
touching become highlighted with a colour.

Double-click
Two distinct touches on your mouse button in quick
succession will open the file represented by an icon.

Click and hold
With the pointer over a menu heading, press the
mouse button down but don't release it. This action
is used to reveal a pull-down menu and other
elements. Keeping the mouse button held down,
move the mouse and you'll see that items in the
menu become highlighted as the pointer passes
over them. Release the button only when you have
selected the option you want. To not select anything, move the pointer away from the menu and
then release the button.

Drag

Click down on your mouse button, but don't release it – this gives you control over the item you've selected. You can then move the item where you want – you'll see a "ghost image" of it trail your movement – and release the mouse button to finish. If you change your mind and want the item to stay where it was, you can drag it to the menu bar across the top of the screen and *then* release the mouse button. The item will return to its original location.

Drag and drop

Drag an icon until it's directly on top of another icon, which will then become highlighted to confirm the action. You'll use this action to open a document in a specific application, for example. Release the mouse button once the second icon is highlighted.

Selecting multiple items

You're not restricted to selecting just one item at a time, either. To select more items after you've highlighted one in Icon view, you can hold down the Command key, then click on the other items you want. In List view or Column view, you have even more flexibility. Select one item, then hold down Command to select more items one by one. Alternatively, if you select one item, then hold down Shift and click on another item, this selects both the original item, the second item you clicked on, *and* all the items in the list between the two.

Yet another way of selecting multiple items is to draw a "marquee" around them: instead of clicking on an item, click and hold in some blank space near the items you want, and then move the pointer to draw a box around the items (you'll see a shadowed box as you move the mouse pointer). Any items included within the box you draw will be selected. You can combine all these methods of selecting items too: draw a marquee around a group of items, then Command-click to deselect the items you don't want included.

Mac upgraders

Note that in Mac OS X you now hold down the Command key, not the Shift key, to make multiple separate selections. Hold down the Shift key to select a whole range of items.

II Welcome to Mac OS X

Whether you've bought a new Mac with Mac OS X installed on it or you're adding it onto your current Mac, here's how to ensure a hassle-free setup.

4 Before You Start

For the smoothest possible installation of Mac OS X, there are several issues you should check out before you even insert a CD. The first is obviously to make sure you've got the OS. If you have bought a new Mac since April 2001, you will already have Mac OS X installed on your hard disk, even if it is not currently running. If so, you can go straight to "Setting up Mac OS X" on page 43 and skip this chapter and the next, where we focus on installing Mac OS X onto Macs that don't have it already.

See also

We look briefly at developer tools in the Guided Tour "How Mac OS X Works" on page 215. You can find more information at the Website **www.apple.com/ developer/**.

If you don't already own it, Mac OS X is available to buy from your Mac dealer or direct from Apple. Visit **www.apple.com/,** and look for your country's Apple site from the list at the bottom of the main page. Then look for the tab at the top of the screen that takes you to the Apple Store for that region. The boxed version of Mac OS X includes three CD-ROMs: one for Mac OS X itself, one for Mac OS 9, and a Developer Tools disc for anyone who wants to create software to run on Mac OS X.

What you need to run Mac OS X

Like other operating systems, Mac OS X won't run on just any computer. You need a Macintosh with a

PowerPC G3 processor or a subsequent processor, such as the PowerPC G4. Machines that have been upgraded to G3 or G4 with processor upgrade cards won't run Mac OS X (at least, not officially).

Apple says these Mac models are compatible with Mac OS X:
• iMac
• PowerMac G3
• PowerMac G4
• iBook
• PowerBook G3 (except for the original PowerBook G3 model; this was sold between November 1997 and March 1998 and had a 250MHz PowerPC G3 processor)
• PowerBook G4

All newer Macs are able to run Mac OS X.

Some people have succeeded in getting Mac OS X to run on older PowerPC-processor-equipped Macs, and there is a program called Unsupported UtilityX to help you do so. You can download it from **www.versiontracker.com**. However, Apple doesn't offer any technical support for the use of Mac OS X on models other than the ones listed above, so you run it on older models at your own risk.

In addition, Apple recommends that your Mac has 128MB of memory installed; we'd advocate even more, say 192MB or 256MB, to make Mac OS X run more smoothly. Contact your Mac dealer for details of the type of memory you should get for your model. All the recommended Mac models have more than enough hard disk capacity to store Mac OS X once it's installed, although you may need to clear some space by removing non-essential files, such as documents or unused applications. Installations of Mac OS X will take up between 1GB and 1.2GB of hard disk space, depending on the Mac you own, and you may need additional space to update your older Mac OS to version 9.

Transferring your Internet settings

If you already have Internet access in the location
you're using your Mac, you should make a note of
your Internet and network settings: you will need
to re-enter them as you set up Mac OS X.

Mac OS

If you've been using an older version of the Mac
OS, these are the settings you need. You may have
more than one Internet account or e-mail address,
of course; if so, you need to note each configuration
separately and re-enter the settings for each.

From the **Remote Access** Control Panel:
• Phone number
• User name
• Password
  (The settings may be empty.)

From the **TCP/IP** Control Panel:
• IP Address
• Subnet mask
• Router address
  (These three settings may all show "Will be
  configured automatically".)
• DNS addresses
• Search domains

From your **e-mail program**, such as Outlook
Express or Netscape:
• Account name (for your reference only)
• Your name (this is the name people see when they
  receive a message from you)
• User name
• Password
• Incoming or POP mail server
• Outgoing or SMTP mail server

In Outlook Express, you will find these details
under **Tools > Accounts**; select your account from
the list to view the settings.

In Netscape Messenger or Netscape Mail, you will find these details under **Edit > Preferences**; open the Mail & Newsgroups category and refer to the Identity and Mail Servers areas.

Microsoft Windows

If you have been using Microsoft Windows, these are the settings you need to note down:

From your Dial-Up Networking Connection (Open **My Computer/Dial-Up Networking**, then double-click on the relevant connection):

- User name
- Password
- Phone number

From your TCP/IP Networking Protocol (Open **My Computer/Dial-Up Networking**, then right-click on the relevant connection and select Properties from the menu; click the Server Types tab and then the TCP/IP Settings button):

- Your IP address
- DNS addresses (shown as Primary DNS and Secondary DNS

From your e-mail program, such as Outlook Express:

- Account name (for your reference only)
- Your name (this is the name people see when they receive a message from you)
- User name
- Password
- Incoming or POP mail server
- Outgoing or SMTP mail server

In Outlook Express, you can find these details by looking under **Tools > Accounts**, then clicking on the Mail tab. Select your account and click the Properties button to open the account box, then see the General and Servers tabs for the information.

5 Installing Mac OS X

You're now ready to start installing Mac OS X.
There are two approaches you may want to
consider. If you've been using a Mac for a while,
you're likely to own an extensive library of software, not all of which will have been converted for
Mac OS X. Mac OS X uses its "Classic environment"
to run these, which relies on Mac OS 9.1 (or a
subsequent revision beginning with 9) to run. The
latest revision available at the time is supplied in
the Mac OS X package or is already installed when
you buy a new Mac.

See also

We look at Classic in
the Guided Tour "Living
with the Legacy" on
page 201.

There may also be instances where you need to exit
Mac OS X entirely and restart in Mac OS 9, because
a given program won't function correctly in Classic
or you need access to a device that Mac OS X
cannot yet recognise. Perhaps a Mac OS X driver
has not yet been written for your scanner, for
instance. (Check the maker's Website for one.)

If you don't expect to use Classic or Mac OS 9 often,
follow the basic installation procedure below. If you
believe you will be using Classic or Mac OS 9
regularly, consider the advanced installation
procedure that follows. The basic approach will still
work if you don't want to attempt the advanced
procedure, though.

Basic installation

This procedure is better if you don't expect to use Classic regularly.

1. Make sure you have a functioning copy of Mac OS 9.1 (or a newer revision) on your hard disk. If you have an older version, use the Mac OS 9 installation CD-ROM to update it.

2. Insert the Mac OS X installation CD-ROM and run the Installer. This program will automatically restart your Mac and use the CD-ROM to commence installation. The installation process may take half an hour or so, depending on the Mac you own. Once it's finished, your Mac will restart after a few seconds and launch Mac OS X.

Quick tip

Before you start, copy all the data on your hard disk onto another medium, such as an external hard disk or CDs. This should include the contents of your current System Folder. You can then restore anything you find you need from this backup.

Advanced installation

This procedure is better if you expect to use Classic often or need to restart in Mac OS 9 from time to time. The end result will be that your hard disk space will be split into two "partitions". One partition will hold a Mac OS 9 System Folder; the other will hold a second copy of Mac OS 9, plus a copy of Mac OS X. The advantage of this setup is that you can configure the stand-alone copy of Mac OS 9 the way you want it to behave when you restart in Mac OS 9, and the other copy the way you want Classic

Any iMac can run Mac OS X to its fullest extent, along with the Mac models that have gone on sale since, such as the iBook and the PowerMac G4. Photo courtesy of Apple.

to behave when you run Mac OS X. For example, you can reduce the number of Extensions and Control Panels in your "Classic" version of Mac OS 9 so that it runs quicker and uses less memory, but retain those Extensions and hardware drivers for the stand-alone version. You might also keep different sets of fonts in each.

Manipulating the System Folders in this way does require knowledge of how Mac OS 9 works, so stick to the basic installation if you're unfamiliar with it. Attempt this procedure using only Mac OS 9.1 or newer for both System Folders, which makes it easy to switch between operating systems.

Quick tip

Before you start, make sure you have backed up everything on your hard disk onto another medium, such as an external hard disk or CDs. This is vital if you choose to follow this "Advanced installation" procedure, because this procedure will erase everything from your hard disk.

1. Insert the supplied Mac OS X installation CD-ROM and run Install Mac OS X; this will restart your Mac and run the installer application direct from the CD.

2. When the first screen appears, inviting you to select a language, you should instead select **Installer > Open Disk Utility**. This will run the Disk Utility program direct from the CD.

3. You can see at least two storage volumes in the list to the window's left. (One icon is for the CD you're using.) The largest volume of all is your hard disk; select this, then click on the Partition tab to the right.

4. You can see a diagram representing your hard disk. Confirm you have chosen the right volume by looking up its label in the Name field. Now click the Split button to divide your hard disk space into two. Drag the bar between the two to change their relative sizes; one option is to make the lower of the volumes in the diagram as small as possible (about 1.5GB), then use this later to store your Mac OS 9 System Folder. All your applications and documents will be held, along with the Mac OS X and Classic System Folders, on the larger volume.

5. Click in turn on each partition within the diagram, then give it a name. Make sure the format is Mac OS Extended and that the option Install Mac OS 9 Disk Drivers is ticked.

6. Click on OK. This will wipe your hard disk and divide it in two partitions of the sizes you've chosen here.

7. Quit Disk Utility, then quit Installer, which will restart your Mac. As the Mac is starting up, use your Mac's eject button to pull out the Mac OS X CD and insert your Mac OS 9 disc. The Mac will start up using the System Folder on this CD.

8. Install Mac OS 9 onto the smaller of your two volumes; this is the copy you will later use when you are running natively in Mac OS 9. When the Mac restarts, hold down the **C** key on the keyboard to start up from the CD once more.

9. Install Mac OS 9 onto the larger volume; this is the version you will use to support Classic. It's essential that you install this copy before you install Mac OS X. The Mac will restart again; this time, let it run its course and start from the System folder on your hard disk.

10. Insert the Mac OS X installation CD-ROM and run Install Mac OS X. This program will automatically restart your Mac and use the CD-ROM to commence installation.

Quick tip

If at any time in the future you need to make your Mac start up using the System on a CD, such as the OS X install CD-ROM, simply hold down the **C** key on your keyboard as the Mac restarts. (Make sure the CD in the drive has a System folder on it!) On newer Macs (but not some older models), hold down the Option key as the machine starts up and you're presented with a dialogue box where you can select which System folder to start up with.

Installation decisions

After you've chosen between the basic and the advanced procedure to prepare your Mac for Mac OS X, installation itself is quite straightforward. You're first asked which language you want instructions to appear in, and then have a couple of screens of information to read through. The first reminds you of the hardware requirements we looked at in the previous chapter; the second is your legal licence for Mac OS X. You must agree to the terms to continue.

The next screen is headed "Select a Destination". If you used the basic procedure above, you probably have just one choice, so click on this volume. If you used the advanced procedure, you have two volumes; click on the larger one. Ignore the option to erase and format the disk, as there's a copy of Mac OS 9 on the disk that you want to keep. Click the Continue button.

The next screen is headed "Easy Install". Click on the Custom button to see a list of optional packages that you can opt not to install. We recommend installing the BSD Subsystem and Additional Print Drivers packages, since these add important features to Mac OS X. You may want to untick some of the language options if you have no plans to run your Mac in those languages.

You can now click the Install button. The installation process may take half an hour or so, depending on the Mac you own. Once it's finished, your Mac will restart after a few seconds and launch Mac OS X.

6 Setting Up Mac OS X

Quick tip

The bewitching snatch of music introducing the Setup Assistant is the Richard Dorfmeister remix of "Sofa Rockers" by the Sofa Surfers. It's available on the Kruder and Dorfmeister compilation CD The K&D Sessions.

The very first time you run Mac OS X, it automatically launches a Setup Assistant, so that you can enter in some key details about how you want the operating system to work. You must complete the process before Mac OS X will work.

Which language?
The first question you're asked is which language you want to use. Choose from the pull-down menu.

Keyboard
The keyboard configuration you choose is related to the language you're using. Make sure you choose the country that corresponds with where you bought your Mac, otherwise pressing some keys may not give you the character you expect. US and British keyboard configurations have currency symbols in different places, for example.

Registration
You're then asked for some basic personal details, such as your name, address and e-mail address. This is purely an Apple Computer marketing exercise to build up a register of its customers. Apple asks if you would like to receive e-mail newsletters from the company, and gives you a chance to read its privacy policy, which states that

it will not pass on your details to other parties without your consent. If you find all this intrusive, it's important to realise that you are not obliged to enter any personal information. While you must fill in the form, you can enter gobbledygook if you prefer and still move on the the next stage. It doesn't matter what you enter, and it won't affect your use of Mac OS X at all. That said, though, the newsletters are quite interesting and let you know about Mac OS X features and software you might not come across otherwise. The decision is yours.

Create your account

The Setup Assistant will now ask you to create a user account. User accounts are designed for Macs that are accessed by more than one person: each individual can have their own user account, which lets them set up the look and behaviour of Mac OS X as they prefer, without interfering with how the others like it. Documents within each user account are also protected from the other users, until you decide you want to share them. You may eventually end up with several user accounts on your Mac, but for now you're asked to create just one so the Mac can get started. If you're the only person likely to be using your Mac, you still have to create a user account, but just the one.

The choice of who this account should belong to is important, because this initial user account will give its owner more control over Mac OS X than other accounts might. Some users can be made "Administrators", with the right to manage the overall operating system – installing new software, for example. The initial user account you create now is always set to Administrator level, so make sure it belongs to someone you trust! You can delete this entire account later if you choose, but you can't remove its Administrator privileges. If you know all the people who'll be using your Mac, you might want to discuss with them whether you wish to maintain separate user accounts, and who is capable

See also

We explore user accounts and privileges in more detail in the Guided Tour "Sharing Your Mac" on page 155.

enough to enjoy Administrator privileges. There can be more than one Administrator on a Mac, and you can grant or remove Administrator privileges on any account, other than this first one.

To create your first user account, you need to provide two forms of your name. The long name is your account's official name, but you'll also need to provide a short version of that name – no more than eight characters long. This is because some of the tools Mac OS X employs will work only with account names of that length. The short name will also be the one you'll see in the Finder when you're working with files, so make sure it's easily recognisable to you and other users.

You're also asked to provide a password to prevent others from logging into your user account. If that's a real concern, make the password difficult to guess. The easiest passwords to guess are those based on the names of family members, friends or pets, because that's what most people use.

Quick tip

If you're concerned about your Mac being stolen, use the password hint field to type in your contact phone number and perhaps an offer of a reward for the Mac's safe return. Anyone using the stolen Mac who fails to enter the right password will then see this message and be able to contact you.

You also have the option of creating a hint in case you forget your own password. If you're later asked for your password and enter it incorrectly three times, the hint you type in here will be displayed. Anyone else attempting to guess your password will eventually see this hint, so don't make it too obvious.

Get Internet ready

You're also asked at this point if you already have a form of Internet access you want to set up. If you don't yet have Internet access, skip this part and move on to the next. If you've been using the Net in Mac OS 9 or an older version or in Microsoft Windows, see the earlier chapter "Before You Start" for a list of the settings you should have noted down for this moment.

You're first asked how you connect to the Net: through a modem, an office Ethernet link or a broadband setup such as DSL or cable. Once you've picked the appropriate answer, Mac OS X asks you for the basic Internet settings it needs to make the connection. These include your user name and password; you may also be asked for details specific to your Internet connection, such as the service provider's access phone number if you're using a dialup (modem) connection, or your IP address if you're using Ethernet. If you use a modem, you'll also be asked to choose the model you're using. Since every Mac that Mac OS X is compatible with has its own built-in modem, that's what most people use, and you should find that the correct settings are already in place. Use the pull-down menus to change your modem if that isn't the case.

Your iTools account

Once you've created your initial user account, you'll be given the chance to set up an iTools account for that same user. iTools is a free service from Apple Computer that gives you access to several Internet-based tools, including an iDisk area where you can store files you can share with others over the Internet, plus a free mac.com e-mail address. iTools works with Mac OS 9 as well as Mac OS X, but is closely integrated into the latter.

If you don't have Internet access, skip this part and move on the next.

If you already have an iTools account, you can simply enter the member name and password that you already have. Otherwise you have the option to create an iTools account from scratch, which will be registered once you connect to the Internet for the first time under Mac OS X.

If you have Net access but have never registered an iTools account, you can do so now. Enter the user name and password you'd like, and Mac OS X will

Quick tip

If your present Internet access is through AOL, your Internet settings will not work directly with Mac OS X. Treat the Setup Assistant as though you have no Net access, then use the Mac OS X version of AOL to create your Internet connection later. There's more information on AOL in the Guided Tour "Mac OS X Online" on page 169.

See also

We look at the iTools features built into Mac OS X as part of the Guided Tour "Mac OS X Online" on page 169.

use the Internet details you've entered to check
whether the user name is available.

Connect to Apple

Mac OS X now uses the Internet account details
you've entered to connect to the Net and forward
the personal details you typed in. It will try again
another time if it can't make the connection now.
You also get the chance here to set your Mac's clock.
Mac OS X will link to an accurate clock on the
Internet to get the right time.

Setting up e-mail

The next-to-last option is to set up your e-mail
account. If you entered your iTools account details
earlier in the welcome process, you already have a
mac.com e-mail account set up in Mac OS X, but
you can decide to add another one now. This will
typically be the e-mail address you got through
your Internet service provider or, if you're using
your Mac in an office, your work e-mail address.

If you were already accessing the Internet through
an older version of the Mac OS, this is where more
of the details you should have noted down during
the chapter "Before you start" will come in handy.

Where you live

Nearly done now. The final chore is to pick the
global time zone in which you live, so that the Mac
can display the right time, and adjust it for seasonal
variances such as British Summer Time (BST) or
Daylight Savings Time, where applicable. Just click
on the map in the region of the world where you
live, then confirm your country in the pull-down
menu underneath. Now Mac OS X is ready to start
up for the first time.

Quick tip

If you're based in Britain,
the pull-down menu will
initially show Greenwich
Mean Time (GMT). If you
use the menu to select
United Kingdom,
however, your Mac will
automatically switch
between GMT and BST.

7 Exploring Mac OS X

In this chapter, we'll take a few minutes looking around Mac OS X before we explore the operating system more thoroughly in later chapters. First, though, you must log in as Mac OS X starts up. You can see a box listing the user name you chose during installation. Enter your password to continue into the full Mac OS X.

First impressions

Pretty, isn't it? As soon as you start Mac OS X for the first time, you can see how delightful it looks. There are four key elements on the screen the first time you start: the open window showing your storage volumes, the Dock at the bottom, the menu bar at the top, and the Desktop, which is the pattern that everything is resting on.

The arrow hovering on the screen is your mouse pointer and reproduces the movements you make with your mouse. Start by moving your mouse down to the Dock. As you move along the icons, you can see the name for each icon appearing above it. There are two sections to the Dock: the left holds applications and the right holds other items, such as documents, folders and windows. Right now there's

See also

Explore each of these elements in the next few chapters.

an icon labelled "Apple – Mac OS X": this is a direct
link to the Mac OS X Website, where you can find
information and extra applications to enjoy.

Right now, though, click on the iMovie application
icon. You can see the icon bouncing briefly as the
application starts.

Exploring applications

As iMovie starts, you can see that new windows
open up and that the headings in the menu bar
change. The Dock remains present, however. If you
click on the Finder icon on the far left of the Dock,
you can see the screen switch back to the previous
view, with the Finder window still open. If you
look carefully in the Dock, you can see arrows
underneath the Finder and iMovie icons: these
indicate that the applications are active, even if
you can't see all of them.

Click on the iMovie icon and click the Quit button
in the project box in the middle of the screen.

Now we're going to open an application that isn't in
the Dock. Move your mouse to the toolbar in the

See also

You'll be able to try the
Mac OS X Website icon
once you set up your
Internet connection, a
topic covered in the
Guided Tour "Mac OS X
Online" on page 169.

This is the first sight you
see of Mac OS X in
action, with hard disk
and network volumes
presented in a Finder
window. Double-click
any volume to see its
contents.

open Finder window, and click on the Applications icon there. The window view will change to show a list of applications, including the ones that you can still see in the Dock. Find the icon in the window for TextEdit and double-click on it to start the program. You can see a new icon appear in the dock to represent TextEdit.

Quick tip

If you can't see TextEdit in the Applications window, drag the blue scroll bar on the right to move down the list.

TextEdit is a basic word processor. It presents a blank window into which you can type. If you click in the window, your mouse pointer changes shape, appearing now like a thin vertical bar. This is a text cursor and indicates that you may now type in the area you have selected. If you move the text cursor out of the TextEdit window, over the dock or the Desktop for example, you can see the usual mouse arrow reappear.

Next we're going to use a menu option to quit this application. Go to the **TextEdit** menu and select **Quit TextEdit**. (Usually we write this as **TextEdit > Quit TextEdit**.) This returns you to the Finder. You may have noticed that the menu immediately to the right of the Apple logo in the menu bar changes to reflect the application you're using at the time; it should now show Finder.

This is a typical Home area, with ready-made folders to store your documents, movies, music and pictures.

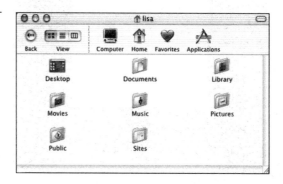

Homeward bound

Time to explore what you can do with your open
window. First, click and hold on the title bar at the
top of the window, then move the mouse: the
window will follow your mouse movement.

We're now going to look inside your Home area,
which you can later use to store all your documents
and personal files. Click the Home icon in the
Finder window toolbar, and the view will change
again to show a series of folders. you can double-
click any of these to see what's inside. If you do
this, click the Back arrow in the toolbar to go to
your Home area again – or you can click the Home
icon once more.

Once you've had a look around, click the Computer
icon in the toolbar, which restores the view you
started with. It's time now to explore Mac OS X
in more detail.

Quick tip

You might want to keep
your Mac on and follow
the guide on your screen
as you read, but if you
prefer to shut down your
Mac for now, select
Shut Down from the
Apple menu.

III Elements of Mac OS X

Most applications in Mac OS X make use of the same visual elements. Master these and you can start using Mac OS X to the full. In this section, we explore the Desktop, the Dock, the menu bar, windows and other tools.

8 Windows in Mac OS X

Many applications present windows – frames containing information for you to view or change. The window might hold a word processing document, an image or, in the Finder, the files you're using. Every window has common elements which behave in the same way, whichever application you're using:

Title bar

Running across the top of the window, this presents the name of the file you have open. If you click and hold within the title bar, you can move the window around the screen. If you click on the document name while holding down the Command key, you'll see the folder "path" – the precise location of the file in the hierarchy of folders on your hard disk.

Quick tip

The symbols that appear in the buttons when you move the mouse over them hint at their function: a cross for Close, a minus sign for Minimize and a plus sign for Maximize.

Window buttons

The top left of the window has three small buttons, coloured red, yellow and green respectively. Although these traffic-light colours might suggest that the buttons work in a sequence, their functions are in fact entirely distinct.

The Close button

The red button closes the window. When
appropriate – for example, if you've made some
changes to the word processing document you have
open – you will be asked if you wish to save the
material contained in the window. If you have more
than one window open (you've been working on
several documents at once, say), you can close *all*
open windows at once by holding down the
Option key when you click in the red button
of the frontmost window.

The Minimize button

The yellow button shrinks the window into the
Dock, clearing the screen so you can view other
information but keeping its contents intact. In fact,
you can still see how the window looks in the Dock.
To bring the window back into full view, just click
on its icon in the Dock: if you have switched
application, this also takes you into the application
associated with the window.

The Maximize button

The green button grows the window, making it
take up as much room as it needs to show you
more of the information it's storing. Click on the
green button again to take the window back to
its former size.

Toolbar

Some windows contain a toolbar, a line of icons or
labels giving you access to important functions.
Have a look at the toolbar in the Finder or in
Internet Explorer, for example. The application
usually enables you to customise the toolbar,
moving icons to different positions or adding or
removing options. Often you can hide the toolbar
completely. Look for a menu option with a name
like "Customize Toolbar" in your application.

Quick tip

A small dot inside the
red button means
changes have been
made to a document
since you last saved it.
You'll get the chance
to save these changes
when you choose to
close the window.

Quick tip

Minimized windows in
the Dock will disappear
if you quit their host
application, but you'll get
the chance to save them
first if necessary.

Quick tip

Window buttons work
even if their window is
behind another one,
letting you clear windows
out of the way by closing
or minimizing them.
Move the mouse pointer
over the button set you
want to use; when they
show their usual colours
rather than being
bleached out, you can
click on the buttons.

Scroll bars

If the space the document needs to show its contents extends beyond the dimensions of the window, you'll see scroll bars running along the bottom or down the right-hand side. The scroll buttons within the bar indicate the visible portion's position within the whole document. You can navigate through the document using the scroll arrows within the scroll bar or by clicking within the bar itself to advance the scroll button in that direction. If you click and hold on the button itself, you can drag it to move it through the document for speedy navigation.

You can choose whether to have the scroll arrows at each end of the scroll bars or grouped in the bottom-right corner. Open System Preferences and click General. There, you can also choose the effect that clicking in the scroll bar has.

Resizing control

In the bottom-right of many windows is a control for changing the window's dimensions. Click and hold the control, then manoeuvre it to get the window the size and shape you want.

Contextual menus

Many windows reveal a menu if you click in a blank area while holding down the Control key. These are called contextual menus, since their options change depending on where the mouse is when you click. Experiment to see what shows up in different application windows. Contextual menus also work with icons on the Desktop, and on the Desktop itself. Some items in the Dock, such as the Trash, display a contextual menu if you click and hold on them *without* holding down Control.

Quick tip

When a window has a toolbar, you may also see a toolbar button in the top-right of the window. Click on this to hide the toolbar from view, and again to restore its presence.

Windows users

Control-clicking in Mac OS X is equivalent to the use of a PC's right-hand mouse button, which calls up menus in Microsoft Windows. This is because mice supplied with Macs have only one button. You can buy two-button mice to use with Macs, and if you don't install a driver for the mouse, Mac OS X will treat the right-hand button press as a Control-click, enabling you to access contextual menus in the same way you're used to in Windows.

Making a selection

You may want to select a piece of material from a larger document so that you can perform an action only on your selection – changing the typeface of some text, for example, or deleting it. You can select material – typically text – by highlighting it; then perform the task by selecting the relevant menu option or keystroke.

There are several ways to highlight text, although not every technique works in every application. You can position your cursor at the beginning of the text you want to select, then drag it down until you reach the end of the selection you want. You should see a colour washing over the selection. If you overshoot and select too much, you can move the mouse back up a document, as long as you keep the mouse button held down throughout the entire action. Release the mouse button when you've made the selection.

There are several precision selection techniques:
• A double-click selects an entire word.
• A triple-click selects an entire line.
• A quadruple-click selects an entire paragraph.

Quick tip

To deselect a piece of material, just click elsewhere in your document.

Quick tip

Some applications enable you to drag a selection to another position in the document or to the Trash in the Dock. You may also be able to drag a selection into another document window. Others may enable you to make non-consecutive selections using a modifier key. Consult your application manual for advice.

9 The Dock

Normally ever-present on your Mac screen, the Dock is a colourful row of icons that gives you constant access to the applications, tools and documents you use most often. Just click on any icon in the Dock to activate the file that it represents; if it's an application, you can see the icon bouncing up and down while the application is prepared for use. Although the Dock already contains several icons when you first start up Mac OS X, you're not stuck with this choice – with the exception of the Finder and Trash icons that bookend the entire Dock, which cannot be deleted or moved. Icons in the Dock can represent applications, documents and other windows, folders or other items. You can see arrows under any applications that are active at any moment, even if no windows for that application are visible.

If an application doesn't have an icon in the Dock, one will be added temporarily whenever you open that program. If you want to keep a temporary icon in the Dock permanently, click and hold on the icon

Quick tip

To quickly switch between active applications, hit Command-Tab repeatedly to cycle through these applications in the order they appear in the Dock. Release both keys when you reach the program you want to use.

The Dock gives you easy access to often-used applications, files, folders or even Websites...

to view the list of options, which includes "Keep in Dock". To permanently add new icons to the Dock, open a window in the Finder and locate the file you want to add, then just drag the file icon onto the Dock. The Dock should clear a space for you to release and deposit the file, which creates a new shortcut icon for you to use. You can also move icons within the Dock by dragging them.

To remove any icon (other than Finder or Trash), click and hold it, then drag it out of the Dock. Release the mouse button and the icon will disappear in a playful puff of smoke. It's important to understand that removing a Dock icon does not erase or harm the file to which it refers in any way; you can always add it again later.

Dock secrets

There are several other tasks you can perform with the Dock. To open a document in a chosen application, locate the document in the Finder, drag it onto the application icon in the Dock until the latter is highlighted, then release the mouse button.

Quick tip

See the divider line in the Dock? Applications go to the left of the line, and other files such as documents and folders to the right.

You can place the Dock along the screen bottom or to either side – although not all at the same time as we've shown it here.

To check which documents and other windows you have open in any active application or folder, click and hold on its icon in the Dock; a list will pop up. You can bring any window to the front of the screen, ready to work with, by selecting it from this list. If a program is active, you can quit it using its Dock menu, even if it isn't the application you're using right now.

Quick tip

Use the keyboard short-cut Command-Option-D to quickly hide and restore the Dock. This shortcut works in the Finder and in the majority of applications.

Some applications can provide instant feedback through their Dock icon. If Mail is active, for example, a red circle in its icon shows you how many unread messages you have right now. Some applications offer additional features in their Dock menu: the iTunes icon enables you to skip between songs or play and pause tracks, for example, as well as seeing which song is playing now. (Applications must be active for feedback to work.)

You can also customise the look and behaviour of the Dock through its preferences, which you can access in System Preferences, or by selecting **Dock** from the Apple menu, or by holding down the Control key and then clicking and holding on the Dock divider line. Through these preferences, you can choose whether the Dock rests at the bottom of the screen or to either side. You can hide the Dock

This "Genie" effect is one of two you can choose as a fun animation when you minimise a window into the Dock or bring it out again.

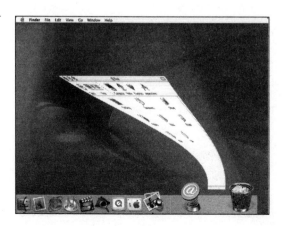

from view, so it slides off the edge of the screen. You can then access it at any time by moving the mouse pointer to the edge of the screen on the side where the Dock is placed. If the Dock is hidden, select Show Dock to give it a permanent presence again.

The Dock will automatically adjust its size to keep every icon visible. If you have too many icons in the Dock to be able to identify them quickly, you can set the Dock to magnify the icon your mouse pointer moves over, so you can see it more clearly. This also gives you several minutes' amusement running the mouse up and down the Dock, making the icons do a Mexican Wave. You can set the overall size of the Dock and the degree to which icons are magnified.

The Finder icon

This is a permanent fixture in the Dock, but works just like any application icon. Click the icon to switch to the Finder, or click and hold to view a menu of available windows.

The Trash icon

When you want to erase a file or other element inside a window, you can drag it to the Trash icon to remove it. You'll use Trash most often to delete files in the Finder, but some applications will let you select material, such as text in a word processor like AppleWorks or a song in iTunes, and drag it to the Trash icon to delete it. (You can just press the Delete key instead, of course.)

Hold down the Control key and click on the Dock's divider to access options for altering where the Dock is placed and how it behaves.

Quick tip

If the Trash has a file in it, you'll see crumpled-up paper in the Trash icon. The bin clears if you empty the Trash.

Dropping a file from the Finder into the Trash doesn't mean it's erased, just removed from its place in the Finder, so you have a chance to rescue the file if you change your mind. To see the Trash contents, click on the Trash icon to open its own window. You can drag any file out of the window to another Finder window. To permanently erase the Trash contents, click and hold on the Trash icon and you'll see a menu with the single option to "empty" the Trash.

Bear in mind that any file held in the Trash continues to occupy space on your hard disk; you won't recover that space until you empty the Trash. If you drag a file from a removable media disk window into the Trash, the file remains on that disk until you empty the Trash. If you eject the disk without emptying the Trash, the file will still be in the Trash the next time you insert the disk.

10 The Menu Bar

In this chapter, we examine the common options you can access in the menu bar, including optional Menu Extras. Running across the top of the screen, the menu bar is a strip giving you access to essential options and information. Some applications, such as games, may hide the menu bar, but usually it's there the whole time.

The contents of the menu bar change depending on which program you're using, so that the options you need at any time are always available. We're listing the menus and options you'll see in most applications, but there are usually other menus too; consult your application manual for assistance. You can select the options listed in menus either by clicking on the relevant menu in the bar and then moving down the list to choose the option, or by using a keyboard shortcut.

Many menu options show a short code to their right: these indicate a key combination you can press to activate that option without using the menu at all. Many people find that using a keyboard shortcut is faster than moving the mouse pointer to the menu and selecting that option, particularly if they've already got their fingers on the keyboard entering text or something, and have at least a few

Windows users

If you use Microsoft Windows, you'll be used to menus being placed inside the particular window you're using. In Mac OS X, the menu always stays at the top of the screen, independent of any windows, but it changes according to which application is active at any time.

Quick tip

Some menu options have an arrow next to them: when you go to that option, a sub-menu appears, and it's this that you use to choose the option you want.

shortcuts committed to memory. Whether a given keyboard shortcut is available, though, is a decision made by the designer of the application you're using: the shortcut for "Hide Others", for example, is frequently not enabled. You'll find the most common keyboard shortcuts given below as we look at the different types of menu and their role in your Mac use.

The Apple menu

The Apple menu lists options that affect the running of your entire Mac. For that reason, it's always available on the far left of the menu bar, regardless of which application you're using. The commands in the Apple menu are:

About This Mac

This option presents a box telling you what version of Mac OS X you're running, as well as the amount of memory you have installed and the type of processor your Mac has.

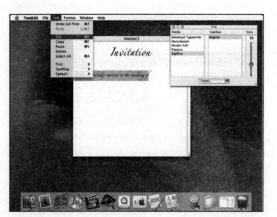

Quick tip

An ellipsis (three dots) after a menu option indicates that you should expect to be asked for more information before completing that task, typically in a pop-up panel that presents extra options or asks you to enter something.

Quick tip

Click on the version number in the About This Mac box to see the operating system's build number, an internal code Apple uses as it creates new versions of OS X.

Whichever application you are using, the menu bar changes to present all the options you need. It's worth learning the indicated shortcuts to save time.

Get Mac OS X Software

This option connects to the Internet and opens a page in your Web browser showing you the latest Mac OS X programs.

System Preferences

This option opens the System Preferences application, which provides many ways to tailor your Mac OS X experience, including how it looks, behaves and connects to the Internet.

Dock

This option provides controls for customising the Dock, such as hiding it from view.

Location

This option lists different network "locations" (connection settings saved as a single configuration), enabling you to quickly switch from one configuration to another.

Recent Items

This option lists the applications and documents you've opened most recently, giving you fast access to anything you've just been working on.

You can choose the number of applications and documents you want listed under Recent Items by opening System Preferences and clicking General. The maximum number of each you can list is 50.

See also

Explore System Preferences in the Guided Tour "Your Personal Mac" on page 143.

See also

Discover more on the Dock in the chapter "The Dock" on page 59.

See also

Discover the benefits of Locations as part of the Guided Tour "Mac OS X Online" on page 169.

Always available for use, the Apple menu enables you to change the state of your Mac – for example sending it to sleep or changing its network Location.

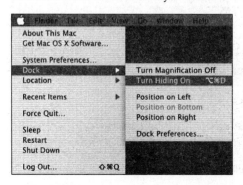

Force Quit

If you're unlucky, an application may sometimes appear not to respond to your prompts, perhaps not opening menus when you click on them or refusing to quit. In these rare instances, use Force Quit to close the offending program. Selecting Force Quit presents a window listing all the applications that are currently running. Select the offending application and click the Force Quit button to close it down, then hit the window's close button to continue. If the entire Mac appears to be behaving strangely or is locking up, you can also Force Quit the Finder with this option. The Finder will automatically restart.

Treat Force Quit as a last resort. It's very rarely that Mac OS X or its applications have problems serious enough to make the operating system seize up. Always satisfy yourself that the apparent unresponsiveness hasn't been caused by something else. If you are connected to the Internet via a modem or to another computer via a network, for example, your Mac can sometimes be slow to respond to your commands because it is focusing on the connection. If you change your mind once you've opened the Force Quit window, just click on the window's Close button, and the Mac will carry on as before.

Sleep

This option puts the Mac into sleep mode, switching off the screen and making the Mac unresponsive to any further commands, without shutting it down completely. This saves energy while you're not using your Mac. If you have a recent Mac, such as an iMac or a PowerMac G4, the power button will pulse gently while the Mac is sleeping.

Restart

This option closes all running applications and reloads the operating system. You will need to log in again.

Quick tip

If you cannot access Force Quit in the Apple menu because the menus themselves appear not to respond, you can use the keyboard shortcut Command-Option-Escape to open the Force Quit window.

Quick tip

If you want to use a different operating system, such as Mac OS 9, use the Startup Disk option in System Preferences to choose which installed System Folder the Mac should start up with before you select Restart.

Quick tip

Hit the space bar on the keyboard to rouse your Mac from sleep.

Shut Down
This option closes all running applications and switches the Mac and its screen off.

Log Out
Keyboard shortcut: Command-Shift-Q
This option closes all running applications and exits your user environment before presenting the Login window, ready for the next user. This is much faster than restarting the machine if you just need to switch between users.

The Application menu

Glance along the menu bar and you won't actually see a menu labelled "Application". That's because this menu always presents the name of the application to which it belongs, so that you can always see instantly which program is active at the moment – something that's not always clear when there are several different windows open. While the on-screen label may change, the Application menu's position immediately to the right of the Apple menu (i.e., second from the left) remains constant, as do the options typically found here.

About [Application Name]
This option gives details of the program you're running right now, such as its version number or credits for the programming team.

The Application menu confirms which program is active by showing its name in the menu bar, and presents vital options for controlling the application itself.

Preferences
This option presents further choices for customising
the application's behaviour or appearance. Typically
the options you find here affect only your use of the
application, and not the experience of others
logging in under their own name.

Services
Present only in selected applications, this option
gives you access to a variety of features and options
that can interact with the application you're using.

See also
Find out more about
Services in the chapter
"Added Extras" on
page 81.

Hide [Application Name]
Keyboard shortcut: Command-H
This option removes all the application's open
windows and palettes, as well as its menus from
view and cycles to the next open application,
without closing any windows or quitting the
program. Any minimised windows in the Dock
belonging to the application are also hidden. No
documents are saved when you select Hide. Click
on the application's icon in the Dock to restore
windows, palettes and menus to view.

Hide Others
Keyboard shortcut: Command-Shift-H
If windows belonging to other applications are
visible behind the window you're using, this option
will hide them.

Show All
If any windows belonging to other applications are
hidden at present, this option will restore all of
them to view, in the background, without any of
them taking over from the application you're using
at present.

Quit
Keyboard shortcut: Command-Q
This option closes the application and cycles to the
next active application (not necessarily the Finder).
If there are any documents with unsaved changes,

you'll be asked if you wish to save them before the application quits.

The File menu

See also

The Finder has its own File menu, but some options behave differently. For more details, see the chapter "Menus in the Finder" on page 107.

Virtually every program you use in Mac OS X provides a File menu, which gives you options for manipulating files belonging to that application. The most common options are given below, although some applications may exclude one or all of them or offer extra options.

New
Keyboard shortcut: Command-N
This option creates a fresh, blank document.

Open
Keyboard shortcut: Command-O

See also

Explore navigation boxes in the chapter "Added Extras" on page 81.

This option opens an existing document so you can make alterations to it. You'll be prompted with a navigation box to locate and nominate the file you want.

Save
Keyboard shortcut: Command-S
This option saves any changes you've made to the document. If the document doesn't yet have a name, you'll be asked to provide one. This option overwrites any document with the same name and

The File menu holds all the options you need for controlling the state of the document you're working on, such as saving it under a new name.

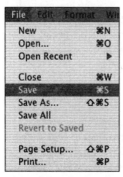

File	Edit	Format	Wi
New			⌘N
Open...			⌘O
Open Recent			▶
Close			⌘W
Save			⌘S
Save As...			⇧⌘S
Save All			
Revert to Saved			
Page Setup...			⇧⌘P
Print...			⌘P

location as the document you're working in.
(Documents in different locations, however,
can have the same name.)

Save As
Keyboard shortcut: Command-Shift-S
This option saves another copy of the document
without affecting the version you opened. Use this
option if you want to make a backup of a file in
another location, or if you want to save the file
under a different name or in a different format.
You'll be prompted with a navigation box to give
the location for the new file, which also gives you
the opportunity to change its name.

Page Setup
This option enables you to match the document
you're working on with the size of the paper in
your printer.

Print
Keyboard shortcut: Command-P
This option enables you to print out the document
you're working on through your printer.

The Edit menu

Like the File menu, the Edit menu is present in
virtually every application you use, and it's always
found immediately to the right of the File menu. Its
options all share the purpose of making a change to
material within the document you're working on.

Undo
Keyboard shortcut: Command-Z
This option reverses the last change you made to
your document, whether it was selecting an option
or typing into it. You can undo an action that
deleted material as well. There are two typical sets
of behaviour for an application's Undo option.
Some programs change Undo to Redo after you

Mac upgraders

If you use an older
version of the Mac OS,
you'll be expecting to
find the Quit option at
the bottom of the File
menu, but its home in
Mac OS X is under the
Application menu, which
is covered earlier in
this chapter.

See also

Find out more about
using printers, and about
using Page Setup, in the
Guided Tour "Go Go
Gadget" on page 191.

See also

As in the case of the
File menu, the options
in the Edit menu are
available in the Finder,
but their behaviour is
different. See the
chapter "Menus in the
Finder" on page 107.

Make a selection in a
window to bring the Edit
menu options to life. You
can cut or copy a
selection before pasting
it in another document.

select it, enabling you to change your mind back
again; others retain the Undo option at all times and
enable you to undo several steps (or even every
step) in a sequence of actions, starting with the most
recent. In the Finder, you can undo all file-related
actions, including copying, moving or trashing a
file, as well as text-related actions such as changing
a file's name. (For more on the Finder, see page 89.)

Cut
Keyboard shortcut: Command-X
If you have selected a piece of material in your
document, you can use this option or Copy to
transfer it to the Clipboard, an invisible, temporary
storage area. You can then use Paste to place the
selection elsewhere. Unlike Copy, Cut deletes the
original selection from your document at the same
time as transferring it to the Clipboard. Cut is not
available until you make a selection. (To remember
the keyboard shortcut, it may help to visualise a
pair of scissors...)

Copy
Keyboard shortcut: Command-C
This option transfers your selection into the
Clipboard without deleting the selection itself. This
is useful when you want to duplicate the selection.

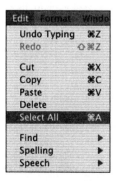

Paste

Keyboard shortcut: Command-V

This option reproduces the contents of the
Clipboard at the position of your cursor in your
document; make sure you place the cursor carefully
before pasting. You can paste the same selection
several times, as long as you don't perform another
Cut or Copy action in the meantime. Paste is not
available until you perform a Cut or Copy. The
shortcut for paste is Command-V. (V is used in
preference to P because it's next to the X and C keys
you use for cutting or copying, and P is already
used for Print. It might help you remember it if you
think of the "V" as a downward-pointing arrow,
meaning something like "paste *here*".)

Clear

This option erases your selection and is not
available until you make a selection. You can also
press the Delete key.

Select All

Keyboard shortcut: Command-A

This option selects all material within a document
(or sometimes within the selected "frame" in a
document, depending on the application). You may
then cut, copy or delete it, or sometimes drag it to
another area.

The Window menu

A regular inhabitant of the menu bar, the Window
menu simply lists the names of the open windows
belonging to the program you're using, enabling
you to switch between them. Some applications
may also use this menu to provide controls for
showing the various palettes that let you work with
the program. There are two further options you
may find:

Close Window
Keyboard shortcut: Command-W
This option shuts the window you're using. If there are any unsaved changes you have made, you are asked if you wish to save the document. You can also click on the Close button in the window.

Minimize Window
Keyboard shortcut: Command-M
This option reduces the window into the Dock. You can also click on the Minimize button in the window's title bar for the same result.

The Help menu

The Help menu's function is simply to provide a constant reminder that you can easily get assistance if you're stuck. There is typically just one option listed under Help, a command to open Mac OS X's Help Viewer and provide the list of reference material supplied for the application you're using.

The Keyboard menu

This menu doesn't always appear. If it is present, what you'll actually see is a flag indicating the region to which your keyboard is set at the moment. Keyboards in different countries have some characters in different positions: if typing a key doesn't give you the character shown on the keyboard itself, you may have the wrong region set (or a foreign keyboard, of course!). To change

See also
Visit OS X's Help Viewer in the chapter "Added Extras" on page 81.

Quick tip
Use the keyboard shortcut Command-? for instant help for whatever you're doing.

Quick tip
To remove the Keyboard menu from view, choose the Keyboard Menu tab in the International area in System Preferences, then make sure that only one region has its checkbox ticked.

If you have several windows open in your current application, the Window menu enables you to switch between them – useful if your screen is too cluttered to see them all.

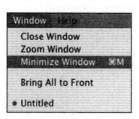

region, go the Keyboard menu and select the
country you want from the list. To get more options,
open System Preferences and select International,
then click on the Keyboard Menu tab.

Menu Extras

While menus hog the left of the menu bar, a set of
icons waits to the right. These Menu Extras provide
quick access to tools or information you may often
need while using your Mac, but would otherwise
have to open System Preferences for. They also
provide constant feedback on the status of the area
they cover. Just click on the Menu Extra you need
to see its options.

AirPort

AirPort is Apple's technology for connecting to a
network wirelessly. If your Mac has an AirPort card
fitted, you can use the AirPort Extra to connect to or
disconnect from a network, or switch network if
you use several. The status icon shows you whether
the connection is active or not. To make the AirPort
Extra visible, open System Preferences and click on
Network. In the Show pull-down menu, choose
AirPort, then tick the checkbox "Show AirPort
status in menu bar".

See also

Find out more about
AirPort in the Guided
Tour "Sharing your Mac"
on page 155.

Battery

Portable Macs can use internal batteries as well
as mains power. On these Macs, the Battery Extra
enables you to check how much time you have
before the battery has no charge left, or to see how
long it will take for it to recharge when you
reconnect mains power. Click on the Battery Extra
to see the status of your battery or to choose
whether to view the remaining power as an
estimated time or as a percentage.

Quick tip

The Battery Extra status
icon indicates whether
you are running off
mains or battery power;
when the outline of the
battery icon turns grey,
the battery is charged. If
your portable is running
off two batteries, you'll
see a double icon in the
menu bar. The battery
bar will change from
black to red when the
charge is running low.

To make the Battery Extra visible, open System
Preferences and click on Energy Saver. Click the
Options tab and tick the checkbox "Show battery
status in menu bar".

Clock

With this Extra, you can view the correct time
constantly, either as a clock face or in digital form.
Click once on the clock to see the date and options.
To show the clock in the menu bar, open System
Preferences and click on Date & Time. Click on the
Menu Bar Clock tab and tick the checkbox "Show
the clock in the menu bar".

Displays

With the Displays Extra, you can check the current
screen resolution and colour settings, then change
them if you wish. You can also control a second
monitor if you have one plugged in. To make the
Displays Extra visible, open System Preferences and
select Displays, followed by the Display tab. Tick
the checkbox "Show displays in menu bar".

PPP

If you connect to the Internet through a modem, the
PPP Extra enables you to log on quickly. The status
icon shows a stream of data coming from a phone:
it's faded out when the modem is inactive and
shown in black when the connection is active. If the
stream is coming from the phone, the modem is
trying to connect; if it's streaming into the phone,
the modem is disconnecting. Click on the PPP Extra
to view the status of the connection or to connect or
disconnect. You can also switch connection if you
have more than one set up. To make the PPP Extra
visible, open System Preferences and click on
Network. In the Show pull-down menu, choose
Internal Modem and click on the Modem tab. Tick
the checkbox "Show modem status in menu bar".
The application Internet Connect also includes a
checkbox to show the PPP Menu Extra.

PPPoE

If you connect to the Internet through a broadband connection, the PPPoE Extra enables you to log on. Click on the Extra to choose the option to connect or disconnect, or to switch connection. To make the PPPoE Extra visible, open System Preferences and click on Network. In the Show pull-down menu, choose Built-In Ethernet and click on the PPPoE tab. Finally, just tick the checkbox "Show PPPoE status in menu bar".

Quick tip

To change the position of any Menu Extra, hold down Command and then click and hold on the appropriate Menu Extra. Move it to the position you want. To remove any Menu Extra, Command-click on that Extra, then drag it out of the menu bar and release: it'll disappear in a puff of smoke.

11 The Desktop

The Desktop is simply the background on top of which every other visual element in Mac OS X sits. You can change the picture it displays or copy files onto it for easy location. To change the Desktop picture, open System Preferences and click Desktop. There are several collections to choose from, including any images you have stored in your Home's "Pictures" folder. You can also select any other folder with images inside. To move a file onto the Desktop, simply drag that file onto an empty area of the Desktop.

See also

Find out about your Pictures folder in the chapter "Finder Basics" on page 91.

The fastest way to make a Mac your own: choose a new Desktop picture from Mac OS X's selection, or find your own image for real individuality.

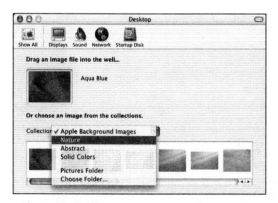

You can also choose to have the visual symbols for storage media in your Mac, such as hard disks, CD-ROMs and Zip disks, shown on your Desktop. To decide which storage media should be represented on the Desktop, go to the Finder and choose **Finder > Preferences**, then tick the checkboxes for "Hard disks", "Removable media" or "Connected servers" as you wish. All these volumes are also accessible through any Finder window, so you don't have to display any of them on the Desktop if you don't want to.

Every user on your Mac has their own Desktop, so you can change yours in any way you like without affecting anyone else's. If you leave any files on the Desktop, others logged in under their own names will not be able to see them.

Quick tip

If you are choosing one of your own images for your Desktop picture, make sure the image is in proportion to your screen resolution, or preferably matches the resolution. This will give you a crisp Desktop background. Check your screen resolution by clicking on the Displays icon in System Preferences, followed by the Display tab.

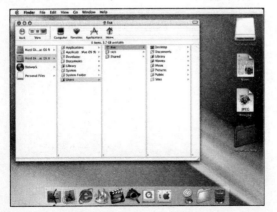

You can use the Desktop to hold documents or folders as well as storage volumes. Users logged into their own accounts can't see your items on their Desktop.

12 Added Extras

In addition to the ever-present elements of windows, the Dock, the menu bar and the Desktop, Mac OS X is able to call up several further features that you can use in many applications.

Quick tip

To open a document, select **File > Open**. To save a freshly-created document, choose **File > Save**. To save a copy of an existing document in a different location or under a different name (or both), select **File > Save As**.

Navigation box

While working in an application, you often want to select a file on your hard disk or other storage volume. Mac OS X's navigation box appears to guide you to the right place. Its most common uses

Use the Open navigation box to move through your folders and select the document you want to work on. You can add regularly-visited folders to your Favorites list.

are to choose a file to open in your application or to choose a location that you want to save your file in. The navigation box's features will vary according to what you're doing.

In the centre of the box, you can see a list of folders and files on your hard disk. Above this is the name of the folder that you're in at the moment. The list includes scroll bars, so you can move up and down the list to find files or folders not immediately visible. You can also scroll to the left to see which folders your current location is nested within, and click on any of the files or folders you see there to change the path you're following. Click on a folder in the rightmost column to view its contents in a new column.

The area showing your current location is actually a pull-down menu listing the most common locations to access, such as your Home, the Desktop or your iDisk. Also listed are folders you've visited recently and Favorites, which are locations you've nominated because you use them so much. You can add a Favorite to this list while you're in a navigation box. Find the folder or file you want to make into a Favorite using the column-based list, then click on it to highlight it. Then click the Add To Favorites button.

If you are opening a file, find the file you want and click the Open button. If you are saving a file, pinpoint the location you want so that it's listed in the pull-down menu label, then click the Save button. You can hit the Cancel button at any time to close the box without doing the task.

Dialogue boxes

These simple boxes may appear from time to time to ask you to confirm an action you've triggered. For example, if you close a document window that

Quick tip

When you first trigger the appearance of the Save navigation box, it appears on the screen in a reduced format. Click on the blue button next to the location pull-down menu to see the larger navigation structure.

Quick tip

To remove any Favorite you've added, go to ~/ **Library/Favorites** and drag the Favorites you no longer need into the Trash. Removing the Favorite will not affect the original folder or file it represents.

Quick tip

Before saving a file, make sure you name it in the text field provided. While you are finding the location to save your file, you can use the New Folder button to add a folder. Choose the area you want the folder to appear in, then click the button to name it.

Quick tip

If one button in a
dialogue or navigation
box is pulsing gently in
blue, you can simply hit
the Return key to trigger
this button rather than
clicking it with your
mouse. If one option is
Cancel, the keyboard
shortcut Command-■
(i.e., Command plus the
full-stop or "period" key)
will normally trigger the
Cancel button.

hasn't been saved, a dialogue box appears to ask
if you wish to save the file. Click the appropriate
button to confirm which action you want to take. In
all dialogue boxes, clicking the Cancel button closes
the box without any action being taken; so in the
box that confirms a save, clicking Don't Save will
close the document without saving any changes,
while Cancel will close the box and return you
to the document.

Palettes and panels

Many applications employ frames that remain
on the screen all the time, floating above other
document windows and containing options or icons
representing features. These palettes or panels are
usually designed specifically for that application,
so you should refer to your application manual for
help. Mac OS X does provide three panels for
applications to use, though: Colors, Font and
Spelling. Whether these are used is the decision of
the application designer, who may prefer to offer
the same features in a different way.

Quick tip

Look in your application
menus for options to
show or hide different
palettes and panels;
some panels also provide
smaller versions of the
Close, Minimize and
Maximize buttons you
normally see in windows.

Colors

This panel enables you to change the colour of a
text selection or other selection. Four buttons along
the top give you a choice of methods for picking the
colour you want: professional designers often prefer
using the tools offered through the Color Sliders
button, for example, because they can enter

Dialogue boxes appear
whenever your Mac
needs you to confirm
what you're doing. This
dialogue pops up if you
try to close a document
without first saving
changes you've made.

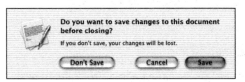

Do you want to save changes to this document
before closing?

If you don't save, your changes will be lost.

Don't Save   Cancel   Save

numerical values to get a precise colour match. Choose your preferred selection method and use the sliders and other controls to pick your colour, then click the Apply button. The item you have selected will change hue to match. Use the small boxes at the bottom of the panel to store colours you want to use frequently: click on your colour in the area above so it appears in the area in the bottom-left, then drag this area into one of the smaller boxes.

Font

This panel enables you to select the font you want to use or to change the font used in a text selection. You can also adjust a font's size or change its styling. You can create collections of fonts to help you find the font you need more quickly.

Spelling

This panel enables you to check for spelling mistakes in the document you're writing. The panel will check each word against its own dictionary, alerting you to any words it finds questionable and offering possible alternatives. You can accept or ignore the recommendation, or ask the dictionary to learn the word for another time. As more applications use the Spelling panel, you'll be able to build up one consistent dictionary you can use in a variety of applications.

Services

Services are options that you may want to access within many different applications, so they're provided in one location under **[Application] > Services**. (The Application menu bears the name of the application you're currently using.) Many, but not all, applications offer access to Services.

Quick tip

To reproduce a colour you can see elsewhere on the screen in the Colors panel, click on the magnifying glass in the panel. Your mouse cursor turns into a magnifying lens itself, enabling you to move around the screen and find the precise dot that holds the colour you want. Click to select the colour, then click Apply to change your selection's colour.

See also

Explore the Font panel in the Guided Tour "Just My Type" on page 209.

Quick tip

You can try out the Font, Colors and Spelling panels in TextEdit, available in the Applications folder. To open the Colors panel, select **Format > Font > Colors**. To open the Font panel, select **Format > Font > Font Panel**. To open the Spelling panel, use **Edit > Spelling > Spelling**.

Quick tip

You can install Services you find on the Internet so they're available through the Services menu. Create a new folder called Services within **~/Library**, then copy the Service you want into this folder. You can find new Services at **www.apple.com /macosx** or at **www .versiontracker.com**.

See also

Get to grips with disk images in the Guided Tour "Go Go Gadget" on page 191.

Many applications are able to use the same colour selection panel, courtesy of Mac OS X. Choose the colour selection method that suits you best.

There is a wide variety of Services available, and you can add more, so the features they offer also vary greatly and are therefore hard to pin down. In general, a Service is able to interrupt what you're doing and carry out a specific action. Many Services are tied into another application on your Mac, enabling you to move a selection from one program to the other while changing its status. The Services included with Mac OS X are:

Disk Copy

The Mount Image option interprets a text selection as a folder path and file name: it looks for the file along that path and attempts to mount it as a disk image, using the application Disk Copy. For example, the text selection "**Users/lisa/Documents/ image.dmg**" will guide Disk Copy from your hard disk through your Users folder and the Home folder "lisa", then to the Documents folder, where it will look for the file image.dmg to mount as a disk image. The file must be an acceptable disk image.

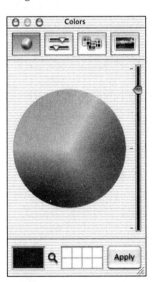

The text selection must include any file extension used in the file name, such as .dmg or .img.

Grab

These options open the application Grab and capture a screenshot (i.e., "take a picture" of the screen) in the format you choose from the list of available options.

Mail

The Mail Text option will create a new message in the Mail application, containing the text selection. The Mail To option will create a new message in Mail addressed to the text selection, which should be in the form of a valid e-mail address. If you see an e-mail address in a document and want to e-mail that person, select the address and use Mail To to create an e-mail.

Make Sticky

This option converts the text selection into a note that opens in the application Stickies, where you can refer to it later.

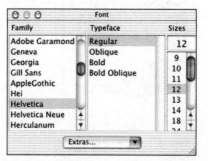

Many applications use Mac OS X's built-in Font panel, although some use their own alternatives. Make a text selection then use the panel to change its font and size.

Summarize

This option will take your text selection and attempt to condense it while retaining the sense of the original. It's best used with long pieces of text. The rewritten material appears in the application Summary Service, enabling you to save or copy the new text.

TextEdit

The Open File option interprets a text selection as a folder path and file name: it looks for the file along that path and attempts to open the file in TextEdit. For example, the text selection "**Users/lisa/Documents/hello.rtf**" will guide TextEdit from your hard disk through your Users folder and the Home folder "lisa", then to the Documents folder, where it will look for the file hello.rtf. The file must be a valid word processor document. The text selection must include any file extension used in the file name, such as .rtf.

Practically every Mac OS X application offers assistance and hints through the Help menu. It's worth browsing for tips even if you're an old hand with the Mac.

The Open Selection option creates a new TextEdit document containing the text selection.

Help Viewer

If you get well and truly stuck trying to do something in Mac OS X, your first move (after checking this book, of course) should always be to look up advice in the Help Viewer, a convenient store of hundreds of explanations, instructions and hints for every occasion. Most applications and the Finder provide a Help menu, which usually has just one option that takes you to a relevant document in the Help Viewer. You may also see a question-mark icon in some windows and dialogue boxes: click on the icon to see information about that window. The Help menu in some applications bypasses the Help Viewer and directs you to the application's own help system; some present pages in a Web browser, for example.

The Help Viewer will always try and present documents that are relevant to what you're doing at the time, but you can search for advice yourself if you need further assistance. Type a word or words connected with what you're doing in the search field at the top of the viewer, then click the Ask button. You can ask complete questions if you prefer, such as "How do I use TextEdit?" You're given a list of topics that the Help Viewer thinks might be relevant; if you spot one that looks good, just click on the title to see the whole document.

You can use the navigation arrows at the bottom to move backwards and forwards through the documents you look up, enabling you to go back to the list if the first document you try isn't what you're looking for. If a document is along the right lines, click the Tell Me More link to see a list of related documents.

Quick tip

Virtually every Mac OS X application offers a help facility – including the Help Viewer itself. While you're in Help Viewer, select **Help > Help Viewer Help** for some great tips on focusing your search down.

Quick tip

Some documents in the Help Viewer are stored on the Internet so they can be kept up to date, so it's a good idea to activate your Internet connection before you enter the Help Viewer.

Quick tip

Click on the question-mark icon in the Help Viewer to see the Help Center, a list of every subject covered by the Help Viewer. Click on a subject link to see a title page with more information. Some applications contribute their own documents when you install them, and these also appear in this list.

IV The Finder

The nerve centre of your Mac OS X experience, the Finder enables you to locate and open applications and documents. Find out how to move, copy and change files with ease.

13 Finder Basics

The Finder is the visual element most associated with your operating system; it provides the controls you need to carry out important everyday tasks, such as opening programs and documents or moving files between folders. The Finder isn't quite like other applications because it's always active, but in other ways you can treat it like any other program. The Finder has its own menus giving access to various commands, as well as windows presenting information – in this case, the location of files stored on your hard disk.

The Finder's icon in the Dock is permanent and cannot be removed. You can always find it at one end of the Dock, opposite the Trash icon. Click on the Finder icon to see a window presenting your files. If a window wasn't already open, the Finder will make a new one when you click on its icon.

Quick tip

You can create a new window by selecting **File > New Finder Window** or using the keyboard shortcut **Command-N** while in the Finder. You can also create a window by double-clicking on any of the storage media icons that appear on your Desktop, providing the Desktop is set up to display them.

Your activities in the Finder will revolve around the windows that present your files and the folders they live in. Here you can open applications or documents or move files from one folder to another. Every Finder window presents standard elements such as the three window buttons and the resizing control, plus a toolbar (though you can choose to hide this – see "Menus in the Finder", page 107).

Storage volumes

When you open a brand-new window, you'll see as
few as two icons within it. These represent the top
of the hierarchy that Mac OS X establishes for your
files: every application, document or other file
you'll use is within one of these areas, but located
on a deeper level (like pieces of paper within
document wallets within a storage box). Each icon
in a new window represents a physically separate
storage area, known as a "volume", for your files.
Hard Disk and Network volumes are always
present, but you may have other volumes displayed
in your initial Finder window. Although they
represent different physical media, all these
volumes store files and behave in the same way
in the Finder.

Hard Disk

The exact label for this icon depends on what name
you've given your Mac's hard disk drive, but we'll
assume "Hard Disk" is close enough. You may have
more than one hard disk icon showing, if you have
either partitioned your single hard disk or have
more than one installed in your Mac.

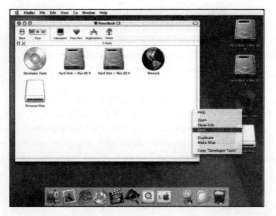

You can open storage
volumes like hard disks,
CDs and removable
media by double-clicking
on their icon in the
Computer area or
on the Desktop.

Network

This is your access point to other computers that may be connected to you in a network. The Network icon is always present.

CDs

If a CD is present in your CD drive, you'll see an icon representing it here. Standard CD-ROMs and rewritable CDs will appear as silver platters; audio CDs add the same Compact Disc logo that's on the music CDs you buy.

Removable storage media

Media such as Zip disks or SuperDisks will display an icon if any are inserted in the relevant drive (if one is fitted on your machine).

Disk images

See also

Discover more about disk images in the Guided Tour "Go Go Gadget" on page 191.

A special case, disk images appear to be separate volumes but are actually files stored on another storage volume, such as your hard disk. If you download a new application from the Internet, it is often packaged as a disk image. Double-click on the disk image icon and it behaves like any hard disk or removable disk, so that you can access its contents.

iDisk

If you have an iTools account, Apple provides a personal storage area on the Internet specially for your files. Your iDisk holds folders and files like any other volume, enabling you or your friends to access your files from any computer with an Internet connection.

To eject any removable volume, click and hold its icon then drag it onto the Trash icon until it's highlighted. As you do so, you'll see that the Trash icon metamorphoses into an arrow-shaped symbol confirming that you're ejecting something rather than deleting it. You can also eject volumes using the keyboard shortcut Command-E or by selecting **File > Eject**.

(Technically you can attempt to "eject" the hard disk that Mac OS X is running on, although the Finder won't let you complete the attempt, and you can't physically eject the hard disk from inside your Mac. It's purely a quirk of Mac OS X treating all volumes in a similar way.)

To view the contents of any volume shown in your new Finder window, double-click on its icon and the window will update to present the volume's contents. If any folders are present, you can then double-click on any of these to view its contents. In this way, you can open any volume and burrow deeper and deeper into its contents until you see the file you need. The window you're using to view all this always shows the name of the folder you're inside in its title bar; if you're viewing the top level of a volume, you'll see the volume name, and if you haven't yet entered a volume, you'll see the name of the Mac you're using.

See also

You can alter many of the standard behaviours of the Finder, so that, for instance, double-clicking on a volume icon opens a new Finder window instead of showing its contents in the current window. See "Menus in the Finder", page 107.

See also

Mac OS X establishes a strict initial hierarchy of folders which cannot be altered, although you can add additional folders. Take a walk through the folder hierarchy on page 98, later in this chapter.

Finder views

The Finder offers three different ways to view the contents of a folder or volume, each with its own benefits and drawbacks:

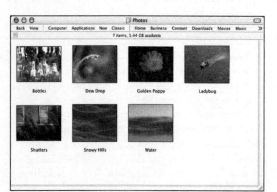

View a folder as icons to see neat rows of files; if they're pictures, use **View > Show View Options** to make the icons big enough to see what each image is before you open it.

View as icons

This is the view you have when you create a new Finder window, and is the least detailed view available. All you can see here are the file names and the icons representing those files.

View by list

This view gives you a straightforward list of all the files in a folder or volume, initially in alphabetical order. The List view provides more details about each file than you get in the Icons view: as well as its name and icon, you can see its size, what kind of file it is and the date you last made a modification to that file. Each such information category has a heading in a bar towards the top of the Finder window. If a volume or folder is included in the list, you'll see beside it an arrow pointing to the right. Click on the arrow to reveal that folder's contents, presented in the same list but indented. Double-click on any folder name or icon to update the view to show only that folder's contents.

View by column

The third view alternative presents the full hierarchy of every volume within your Mac in a single window – fortunately not all at once – and enables you to quickly hop between files at significantly different depth levels. The window

Quick tip

In the List view, click on any category heading to make that the order in which the list contents are presented – i.e., to view files in date order, or by size, and so on. You can also change the order of the category headings themselves (except for Name, which always comes first): just click and hold on a category heading and drag it left or right; the other headings will shift over to make room for it.

View a folder as a list to get instant information on every file it holds. Click on the arrow by any folder to see a sub-list of its contents.

is split into a set of columns. The left-most column always presents a list of every volume within your Mac, including hard disks, the network and any removable media inserted at that moment. Click on any volume icon or name – just a single click rather than the double-click employed in other views – and its contents will appear in the second column; click on a folder in that column and the next column will display that folder's contents; and so on. If any folder or volume has contents waiting to be revealed, you'll see an arrow to the right of its name, as a handy visual cue.

The Column view lets you burrow down through several folders quickly and helps you understand more precisely where a given file is located. But that's just the half of it. When you click on a file rather than a folder in any column, it obviously has no further files inside it to be shown – but every document on your Mac does have contents, such as text or an image, so the following column attempts to present these. Mac OS X is able to recognise many common types of document to the extent that it can present a preview of the document's contents in Column view. So if your file is a photo, you'll see the picture; if it's a movie, you'll get a small window and embedded controls to start playing

Quick tip

In both List and Column views, you can change the width of the columns so you can see longer file names, etc. Click and drag on the "resize tab" at the bottom right of the window to resize all columns equally as you make the whole window bigger; hold down Option and drag on the right-hand side of any single column to change the width of just that column.

Viewing a folder as columns enables you to see what route you took to see this folder. Click on a document file to see an instant preview of its contents.

the video clip. Digital music files such as MP3s also present controls to let you listen to the tune, while word processing documents offer a preview of their first few lines.

With so many different file formats used by programs, Mac OS X isn't able to recognise all of them; but more often than not, clicking on a file in Column view will let you see or hear exactly what you can expect if you open that file in an application. If Mac OS X can't interpret the document, that won't prevent its parent application from opening it when you double-click on the file, of course; but when you click once on it in Column view all you'll see is that file's standard icon in crisp detail. That's also what you'll see when you click on an application. Details such as the file name, type and modification date are presented under the file icon or preview in every end column.

View options

You can refine the icons and list views further by selecting **View > Show View Options** in the Finder. This opens a window presenting choices for affecting the view of your current location, or for deciding what the default view should be – that is, what the view is everywhere except in specific locations where you make changes. Decide first whether the changes you are making should apply only to the current location or globally.

The subsequent options depend on whether your current view is as icons or as a list (you cannot change the Column view). If you're viewing the location as icons, you can change the icon size – useful if you want to get a better look at the "thumbnail" preview icons that some image files use, for example. You can also decide whether to force the icons to fit a set grid arrangement for neatness, and in what order the icons can be arranged: by name, by modification or creation date, by size or by the kinds of files present. Finally, you can ditch the white background in favour or a colour or a picture, which you can use at this point. Use this latter option with caution, though, as it can affect the legibility of file names.

If you're viewing the window as a list, you can use **Show View Options** to pick which category headings should be displayed. If you show any categories with dates, you can use relative dates rather than absolutes – "yesterday" rather than "1st January", for example. You can also elect to show the sizes of folders as well as files, and choose which size all the icons in the list should be.

Directory structure

Mac OS X has a precise hierarchy of folders that it uses, which you can see and move through in the Finder. It's important not to disrupt this by moving folders to different locations.

System
This is the engine driving Mac OS X. You are able to look inside it, but you should never attempt to move or delete files in this folder.

Library
This folder holds important settings and preferences that Mac OS X uses.

Applications
This folder stores all the programs used by Mac OS X. When you install a new software package, it should go here.

Applications (Mac OS 9)
This folder is present if you have Mac OS 9 installed on your hard disk alongside Mac OS X, and holds the programs used by Mac OS 9 and Classic.

Quick tip

If you elect to show the sizes of folders as well as files, be aware that this can take a while to show up, because your Mac has to calculate this by adding up the sizes of all the files in each folder.

Mac upgraders

Not being allowed to move items is a real change in culture from the near-absolute freedom you enjoyed under earlier versions of the Mac OS, but it's important that you adapt to this new way of thinking. We'll look at some of the benefits as we explain the hierarchy.

See also

See how several people can easily share one Mac in the Guided Tour "Sharing your Mac" on page 155.

Users

The most important folder in day-to-day use, this holds the documents and other files made by each person who uses your Mac. Inside, there's a separate folder for each user that you created during installation, plus the Shared folder, which anyone can use.

Inside your Home

Quick tip

Find short cuts to your Home in the **Go** menu or in the Finder toolbar.

Your area within the Users folder is called your Home. It has its own hierarchy of folders inside, designed to store different kinds of documents. While you're not obliged to use them at all – and you can create your own in addition – there are some benefits to following the structure offered by Mac OS X.

Desktop

See also

For more on the concept of Aliases, see the section on the File menu in "Menus in the Finder" on page 107.

This folder stores Aliases of any files you leave on your Desktop. This is personal to you. Other users, when you're logged out and they're logged in, will not see anything that you leave on your Desktop.

Documents

Use this folder to store all your general files, such as word processing documents or spreadsheets.

Each user on a Mac has their own Home, where they can store all their documents and personal preferences for how the Mac should behave when they're using it.

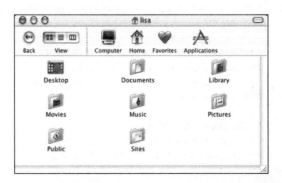

Library

Mac OS X uses this folder to store any preferences that are personal to you, such as the Desktop pattern you prefer to have displayed while you're logged in. It also stores preferences for applications – your own list of favourite Web sites in Internet Explorer, for example, or your e-mail messages in Mail. This way, each user sees their own material even though they use the same application.

Music

Use this folder to store all your digital music files, such as MP3 files.

Movies

Use this folder to store all your video clips, such as QuickTime movies or iMovies.

Pictures

Use this folder to store all your images, such as digital camera photos or clip art. Mac OS X's Image Capture application, which transfers images from your digital camera to your Mac, automatically deposits images in this folder. Some other applications assume that you keep your images here; for example, some screen savers will refer to the Pictures folder for source images.

Public

This is the link between you and other Mac users, whether they're sharing the same Mac or are linked to yours via a network. Other users are not able to view the contents of the rest of your Home, but they can visit this folder to collect any file you leave here, or to deposit a file they want you to see.

Sites

Use this folder to store your HTML documents for reading in Web browsers. If you enable Web Sharing, others on your network will be able to see the pages inside this folder automatically.

See also

Find out more about File Sharing and about Web Sharing in the Guided Tour "Sharing your Mac" on page 155.

14 The Finder Toolbar

Every window in the Finder normally shows a toolbar, giving you fast access to commonly-used options and regularly-visited folders. Every window will show the same toolbar, but you can choose which options to include, as we'll see later. (You can also choose to hide the toolbar if you prefer, as we'll see in the next chapter.)

Toolbar options

These options trigger a particular action.

See also

Discover Mac OS X's CD burning abilities in the Guided Tour "Go Go Gadget" on page 191.

Burn
If your Mac is able to use a CD-writer or rewriter (either internal or external) and you have a blank CD inserted, this option begins the writing process using the files you have copied during preparation.

Connect
Connect to a server – a command we examine in detail in the Guided Tour "Sharing Your Mac" on page 155.

Customize
Open the Customize Toolbar pane for adding or removing toolbar commands and shortcuts.

Delete
Rather than permanently deleting a file, this option moves a selected file or folder into the Trash. If you change your mind, you can recover it from there at any time, or empty the Trash to delete all trashed items permanently.

Eject
This option ejects any removable media, although you must select its icon first.

Find
Opens the Sherlock application so that you can locate an item.

New Folder
Create a new folder, with its title highlighted so you can give it a name.

View
Choose whether the window shows contents as icons, as a list or as columns.

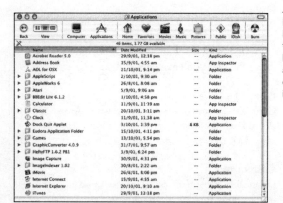

Every window in the Finder includes a toolbar for quickly switching between folders or accessing common options like opening your iDisk or burning a CD.

Folder shortcuts

This set of options changes the view in the window you're currently using. Most of these options are connected with set folders within the standard Mac OS X hierarchy.

Applications
View the contents of the Applications folder.

Back
This option restores the previous view of folder contents that you had in the window. (Like a Web browser's Back button, it takes you back to the previous page – or in this case, window – that you were viewing.)

Computer
View the top level of your Mac hierarchy, with any volumes plus the network.

Documents
View the contents of your Documents folder.

Use the Customize Toolbar option to choose which icons you want in your toolbar; just drag the icon you want from the bottom into the right position in the bar.

Favorites

View the contents of your Favorites folder. We examine Favorites in the chapter "Working in the Finder" on page 117.

Home

View the contents of your personal area in the Users folder.

iDisk

View the contents of your iDisk, your Internet-based storage volume. (Not available if you don't have an iTools account.)

Movies

View the contents of your Movies folder.

Music

View the contents of your Music folder.

Path

This option shows you the complete path of folder levels that you used to reach your current point, letting you choose any point along that route and present that folder's contents in the window.

Pictures

View the contents of your Pictures folder.

Public

View the contents of your Public folder. We examine the Public folder in detail in the Guided Tour "Sharing Your Mac" on page 155.

Customising the toolbar

After you first install Mac OS X, the Finder toolbar
has a default set of options showing the options and
shortcuts you're most likely to want to use. You can
change this selection whenever you like, though. To
change the position of any option or shortcut, drag
it to the location you're prefer it to be in. The
toolbar should clear a space for you to release the
shortcut into. To add a new shortcut for a folder,
just drag its icon onto a blank part of the toolbar,
which will clear space for you to deposit the icon
and create a new shortcut.

To make any other changes to the toolbar, you
need to open the Customize Toolbar pane, which
you can do by selecting **View > Customize Toolbar**
or clicking on the Customize shortcut in the Toolbar
itself, if it's present. When it pops open, the pane
will cover up the Finder window you're using at the
moment; you have to have a window open to
activate the command.

At the top of the pane, you can see the toolbar as it
stands right now. All available shortcuts (we listed
them earlier) are shown; just drag your chosen
shortcut to the rough spot in the toolbar that you
want it, and the toolbar will make room for the new
shortcut. As you add more shortcuts, though, you'll
notice that the roster creeps closer to the right-hand
edge of the window – until ultimately shortcuts
disappear off the side entirely.

You can still access the shortcuts, as an arrow will
appear and provide a pop-up menu of spilt-over
shortcuts. This does defeat the whole point of
having shortcuts, though – they're meant to be a
constant presence for instant access. The lesson is
not to be greedy over your toolbar shortcuts.
Choose the shortcuts you use most often until you

comfortably take up the width of a window, then
stop. Remember the Dock is available for shortcuts
to applications, folders and documents.

If you get in a complete mess moving shortcuts
around and adding extras, you can go back to basics
just by clicking on the image of the default set
shown in the Customize pane. You can also choose
to represent the shortcuts just through their icons or
text names rather than showing both at once. When
you've finished, click the Done button.

Quick tip

To remove shortcuts
from the Finder toolbar,
open the Customize
Toolbar pane, then
simply drag the
unneeded shortcut off
the toolbar.

15 Menus in the Finder

Like every application, the Finder has its own menus, which appear in the menu bar when the Finder is the front application. Bear in mind that there are easier ways to carry out some of the functions listed in these menus, perhaps through the Finder's toolbar or through other techniques covered in the next chapter, "Working in the Finder". If you've read our run-through of menus in the earlier chapter "The Menu Bar" (page 65), you'll recognise many of the menu labels and options in the Finder, and we won't waste your time detailing them again. The options below are those that differ from standard application usage. Any available keyboard shortcuts are also given.

The Finder menu

This menu contains options that are standard for any Application menu, such as "About" and the "Hide" and "Show" options. "Quit" is absent, since quitting the Finder isn't encouraged, and there are two notable further options:

Preferences
This option gives you access to several customisation options. You can choose whether

to show different kinds of storage volume on the Desktop as well as in Finder windows. You can also decide whether a new window should present the contents of your Home rather than the standard Computer view. Checkboxes enable you to decide if double-clicking a folder should open a new window rather than updating the view in the current window, or whether that view should follow the format established for that folder. (Usually you can change the view for each level of a folder.) Finally, you can choose to receive a confirmation warning before you empty the Trash (highly advisable) and force the Finder to show filename extensions at all times (entirely a matter of personal preference).

Empty Trash
Shortcut: Command-Shift-Delete
This option simply erases any files you have in the Trash. Permanently. As in, it can't be undone. You can choose to get a confirmation check by selecting **Finder > Preferences**.

The File menu

The guiding principle of every application's File menu remains true here, but many options are unique to the Finder:

New Finder Window
Shortcut: Command-N
This option opens a fresh window.

New Folder
Shortcut: Command-Shift-N
This option creates a fresh folder at the level that the active Finder window is showing. The folder is automatically named "Untitled Folder", but the name is highlighted so that you can type in a new name immediately.

See also

Find out about filename extensions in the chapter "Working in the Finder" on page 117.

Mac upgraders

The keyboard shortcut for making a new folder in older versions of the Mac OS was Command-N, which now creates a Finder window. Some confusion may result till you adjust to the switch.

Open

Shortcut: Command-O

This option activates a file in the Finder. If the file is an application, the application will launch; if it's a document, the application for that document will open and present that document. If, in either case, the application is already active but not in use, your Mac will switch to that application. If you select a folder, the Open option will show its contents in the active window. You must select a file or folder to use this option.

Close Window

Shortcut: Command-W

This option closes the active Finder window.

Show Info

Shortcut: Command-I

This option opens a window revealing further information about the file you have selected, as well as enabling you to make some changes to its status. You must select a file or folder to use this option.

Quick tip

Use the keyboard short-cut Command-Option-W to close all open Finder windows at once.

See also

Explore the Show Info window in the chapter "Working in the Finder" on page 117.

The Finder's File menu enables you manipulate files, folders and the windows in which the files are presented.

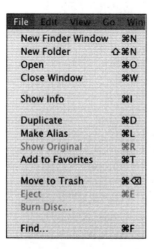

File	Edit	View	Go	Win
New Finder Window				⌘N
New Folder				⇧⌘N
Open				⌘O
Close Window				⌘W
Show Info				⌘I
Duplicate				⌘D
Make Alias				⌘L
Show Original				⌘R
Add to Favorites				⌘T
Move to Trash				⌘⌫
Eject				⌘E
Burn Disc...				
Find...				⌘F

Duplicate

Shortcut: Command-D

This option makes a copy of the file you have
selected, which is placed in the same folder level as
the original. The new file has the same name as the
original with "copy" added at the end. You must
select a file or folder to use this option.

Make Alias

Shortcut: Command-L (for "L-ias" – who says
operating systems can't have a sense of humour?)
This option creates a new file called an Alias, which
links directly to the original; for example, if you
double-click on the Alias or select **File > Open**, the
original file to which the Alias is linked will be
activated. You must select a file or folder to use
this option.

Show Original

Shortcut: Command-R (for "Reveal"?)

This option updates the Finder window to present
the original file linked to the Alias you have
selected. You must select an Alias to use this file.

Add To Favorites

Shortcut: Command-T (for "favouriTe", maybe?)
This option adds to your Favorites a reference to the
file or folder you have selected, enabling you to
choose it from the Favorites list later. You must
select a file or folder to use this option.

Move To Trash

Shortcut: Command-Delete

This option transfers the file you have selected into
the Trash, where you can permanently erase it later
(or retrieve it, if you change your mind). You must
select a file or folder to use this option.

Eject

Shortcut: Command-E

This option ejects a storage volume you have
selected (i.e., removes its icon and also physically

Quick tip

You can quickly tell that
a file is an Alias by the
small arrow in the
bottom-left of its icon.

ejects the media from its drive). You must select a legitimately removable volume, such as a CD or Zip disk, to use this option.

Find

See also

Investigate Sherlock in the chapter "Everyday Applications" on page 125.

Shortcut: Command-F

This option activates the Sherlock application, which enables you to search for files on your hard disk or other volumes, as well as perform other kinds of search.

The Edit menu

The Finder's Edit menu includes the options you might expect from this menu, such as Cut, Copy and Paste, but the menu has two separate sets of actions, which change according to what you have selected. If you select a piece of text in the Finder, typically a file name, the Edit menu options act as normal, enabling you to cut or copy the text from the Finder and paste it elsewhere in the Finder or in other applications.

Quick tip

In the Finder, Cut, Copy and Paste have their usual keyboard short-cuts: Command-X for Cut, Command-C for Copy and Command-V for Paste.

If you select a file rather than its name, however, the options change. Cut is no longer available. Copy changes to "Copy Item", enabling you to copy a reference to the entire file; the accompanying "Paste Item" enables you to place that reference into another location, duplicating the original file. To use the options together, select an original file and select **Edit > Copy Item**, then change the Finder window to the location you want the file to be duplicated

If you click on a file in the Finder, the Edit menu changes to enable you copy that item, ready to paste into another folder.

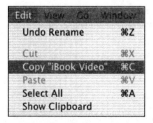

Edit	View	Go	Window
Undo Rename			⌘Z
Cut			⌘X
Copy "iBook Video"			⌘C
Paste			⌘V
Select All			⌘A
Show Clipboard			

into and select **Edit > Paste Item**. The original file
is preserved unaffected.

There are two further options in the Edit menu:

Select All
Shortcut: Command-A
This option selects every file and folder in the
location you can currently see in the Finder. If you
highlight a piece of text in the Finder, though,
Select All then highlights all the available text
in the file name.

Show Clipboard
This option opens a window presenting the contents
of the Clipboard, which holds any text or other
element that you have previously stored through
Cut or Copy.

Quick tip

Remember that the
Clipboard contents are
not permanently saved,
just held there until you
Cut or Copy something
else – but whatever is
held there can be Pasted
any number of times.

The View menu

This menu affects the presentation of files and
folders in the active Finder window. The first three
options enable you to change the window view,
following the choices we set out in the earlier
chapter "Finder Basics" – view by Icon, List,
or Column. There are six further options:

Clean Up
When you view a window as icons, you can place
the files in any position in the window. This option
tidies up the placements you make, lining up the
files in orderly rows. This option is available only
when you view a window as icons.

Arrange By Name
This option rearranges the files and folders in the
active window so that they are arranged in
alphabetical order on a row-by-row basis. This
option is available only when you view a window
as icons.

Hide/Show Toolbar
Shortcut: Command-B (for... er, "toolBar"?)
If the Finder toolbar is visible in the active window, use this option to remove it from view. If the toolbar is not visible in the active window, the option becomes Show Toolbar and reinstates the toolbar. Either option affects only the window that is active right now, not any others in the background, but any fresh windows you create will adopt the same state until you reverse the option again.

Customize Toolbar
This option presents the Customize Toolbar pane in the active window, enabling you to alter the options in the toolbar. Any changes you make are reflected in every window.

Hide/Show Status Bar
The Finder window includes a status bar, resting below the toolbar, which shows the number of items in the location you can see right now, as well as reminding you how much space is available for new files in the storage volume you are currently using. This option hides the status bar if it is currently visible, or shows it if it is not. All Finder windows are affected.

Quick tip

The status bar may sometimes show an icon of a pencil with a line struck through it, on the far left of the bar. This means you cannot make changes to the location you are currently viewing. You can see the icon clearly if you select the System icon on your hard disk, for example.

Special to the Finder, the View menu provides different ways of looking at the contents presented in your windows.

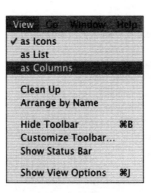

Show View Options
Shortcut: Command-J (for... for "op-Jons"? Oh,
I give up)
This option presents you with a small panel that
enables you to make changes to the window view
in the location you can see right now. Any changes
you make are preserved for the next time you view
that location. We looked at these options in the
earlier chapter "Finder Basics".

The Go menu

This menu is designed simply to switch the view of
the active Finder window to a preset location. The
options included in the Go menu represent locations
you may need to view often:

Computer
Shortcut: Command-Option-C
This view presents every storage volume available
to your computer.

Home
Shortcut: Command-Option-H
This view presents your Home within the
Users folder.

iDisk
Shortcut: Command-Option-I
This view presents your iDisk, the personal storage
area on the Internet available to you if you have an
iTools account.

Favorites
This option presents a sub-menu listing all the
locations you've chosen to add to your Favorites
folder, along with an option to present the Favorites
folder itself. The latter option has the keyboard
shortcut Command-Option-F.

Quick tip

If you're concerned
about security, be aware
that connecting to iDisk
using the Go menu
under OS X 10.1 sends
your password as un-
encrypted text over the
Internet. There are work-
arounds if this matters to
you. See the discussions
about this online at
www.tidbits.com and
www.macfixit.com (in
these two sites, search
for "iDisk via WebDAV"
or something similar) and
**www.opendoor.com/
macosxalert.html**

Applications

Shortcut: Command-Option-A

This view presents the Applications folder.

Recent Folders

This option presents a sub-menu listing the ten most recent locations you have visited in the Finder, enabling you to quickly return to any of them.

Go To Folder

Shortcut: Command-~

This option opens a dialogue box into which you can type the name of a folder; the Finder will locate that folder and show its contents. The option does not work if the folder name you enter is not immediately inside the folder location you are viewing right now.

Connect to Server

Shortcut: Command-K

This option presents you with a dialogue box enabling you to select a server on your local network. If you are not connected to any other computers, the box will be empty.

See also

Find out more about networks in the Guided Tour "Sharing Your Mac" on page 155.

The Window menu

Like the Window menu in other applications, this menu lists all open windows in the Finder so that

Switch your window view from one folder to another quickly with the Go menu, which also enables you to connect to a network server.

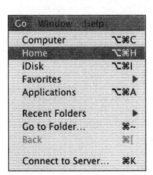

you can choose one to become active. You can also minimize the active window, or bring all Finder windows to the front of the screen, overlapping any windows belonging to other applications.

The Help menu

As usual for the Help menu, there is only one option in this menu, which opens the Help Viewer and offers hints and advice relating to the Finder.

16 Working in the Finder

With the broad structure of the Finder established, it's time now to look at some of the Finder's more discrete features.

Working with files

One of the basic uses of the Finder is to manipulate files, transferring them from one folder to another, removing them, or changing their name, for example. These are the key actions you can take while in the Finder:

Use the Show Info window to get general information about your file – when it was made, what kind of file it is, and much more.

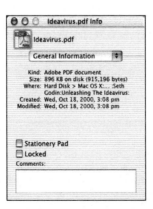

Select a file

Click once on the file icon or name to select it. It will be "highlighted" to show that it is selected. Click somewhere else (either on another file or just a blank area of the screen) to de-select it. To select more than one file, click on the first file you need, then hold down the Command key as you click on further files in turn. To de-select just one file when you have highlighted several, hold down the Command key and click again on the file you want to de-select.

To select a continuous series of files in the List or Columns view, click on the top file of the series you need, then hold down the Shift key and click on the bottom file of the series. This selects both files and all the files in between. You can combine the two: select a series using the Shift, then hold down the Command key to de-select some files in the series or to choose extra individual files.

Change a file name

If you want to rename a file or folder, click not on the icon but on its file name, which should then be highlighted. This enables you to type in the new name. If you want to make only a slight change, click again within the name, and a text cursor should appear where you clicked, enabling you to delete a few letters or add a few more. In OS X, file names can be up to 255 characters long (including extension), and disk names up to 27 characters.

Move a file

You can transfer a file from one folder to another by dragging it between windows or between columns in a single window. You can also drag a file onto a folder to deposit it inside that folder.

To copy a file, leaving the original in place, hold down the Option key as you select the file and drag it to its new location. As already mentioned, you can also use the Copy and Paste commands on files.

Quick tip

Hold down the Control key as you select items in the Finder to see a contextual menu, a pop-up list of options relating to the selected item. You can also see a contextual menu if you Control-click in a Finder window without having anything selected.

Quick tip

Some file names are truncated when there isn't enough space to show the whole name. Hold the mouse cursor over the file name – you don't need to select the file first – and a box containing the full name will appear after a few seconds. The box appears much more quickly if you hold down the Option key at the same time.

Mac upgraders

Note that the modifier key for making multiple selections is different from earlier versions of the Mac OS: after your first selection, hold down Command to select additional separate items; in List or Column view, hold down Shift to select all the items between the first item and the one you click on.

Mac upgraders

In Mac OS X, you can now undo file-related actions in the Finder (such as copying, moving or trashing a file) using Command-Z. You can also still undo text-related changes (like changing a file's name), just as you could before.

Quick tip

Don't name files or folders after the key folders already present in Mac OS X, such as System, Library, Applications or Users. Never begin a file name with a "." (full-stop or period), since Mac OS X uses this to identify some of its most essential files. You cannot use "/" in a file name, since Mac OS X uses this symbol in describing folder paths.

If you're bugged by the three-letter filename extensions shown after many files, you can make them invisible ("hide" them) without stopping the files from working on the PCs that need the extensions.

Any files you transfer between storage volumes are automatically copied rather than moved. You can tell if your action is about to copy a file rather than moving it by the small plus sign that appears in your mouse pointer.

Show Info

You can discover more about a particular file or folder by selecting it, then selecting **File > Show Info**. This opens a window with a pull-down menu of various options, each of which presents information or enables you to make changes to the way the file behaves in the Finder. The options in the pull-down menu vary according to what kind of file you select. The Show Info window can remain open, changing to reflect the details of whichever file you have selected at the time.

General Information

This presents basic information about the selected file, such as its name, its modification date, what kind of file it is and where it's currently located.

Name & Extension

Many files, especially files you download from the Internet, include a three-letter code at the end of their file name, separated from the name itself by a full-stop (period). This is a filename extension

(sometimes called extender or file extension): it's used by some operating systems to establish which application should open the file. The computer's word processor will open any file ending with .doc, for example, while .bin is a commonly-used file compression protocol on the Internet, and so on. Some operating systems can't open a document without a filename extension because they can't work out what application to use, but Mac OS X doesn't actually need extensions itself.

Many people, used to the Mac simplicity of just calling a file whatever they like, find filename extensions irritating, a reminder that other systems are, well, stupid. Fortunately, Mac OS X enables you to keep extensions on every file without actually having to look at them, using the Name & Extension option in the Show Info box. Click the checkbox "Hide extension" and, once you return to the Finder, you'll see that the file name no longer includes its extension. The extension is still part of the file's full name, enabling you to transfer the file to a non-Macintosh computer without problems. Hiding the extension also means you can change the name of the file in the Finder or in a dialogue box, and you will never remove the extension by accident (though if you do delete it from a file's name, this simply has the same effect as ticking "Hide extension").

Languages

This option is shown only when you select an application: it enables you to decide which of the available languages on your Mac this application should use in its menus and other options.

Plugins

This option is shown only when you select certain applications. It enables you to choose which of that application's associated plug-ins, which add extra features to it, should be used when you next run that application. Avoid this option if you're not sure

Mac upgraders

In previous versions of the Mac OS, the OS used colons (invisibly) in paths, so it was not possible to use a colon in a filename. It is now permissible in Mac OS X, but not recommended because this can confuse the Classic environment. In the same way, it is possible to use "/" in filenames if naming files in Classic, but doing so will cause problems in OS X!

Quick tip

You can use the Show Info box to change a file or folder icon. First select the file with the icon you want to use, then select **File > Show Info**. Click on the icon shown in the Show Info window and select **Edit > Copy** (or Command-C). Now select the file whose icon you want to change and return to the Show Info window. Click again on the icon shown here and select **Edit > Paste** (Command-V).

Quick tip

An option under **Finder > Preferences** enables you to choose whether filename extensions should normally be shown or not.

what you're doing with plug-ins, or you could affect the application. Applications offering this option through Show Info include iTunes.

Open With Application

This option is shown only when you select a document. Many people prefer to start applications simply by double-clicking on the document they want to use, which triggers the appropriate application to handle it. Sometimes this scheme can go wrong, though, if your Mac holds several applications capable of opening your document. Maybe it should rely on filename extensions...

Quick tip

You can also "drag-and-drop" to open a selected file using your preferred application: drag the file onto the application's icon (which will highlight in confirmation), then release the mouse button. This is ideal for one-off needs. The Open With Application setting here, though, establishes a permanent link between the file and the application.

Mac OS X has a more elegant solution to the problem. Click on the file you want to open in the Finder, then select **File > Show Info** and choose "Open With Application". This will confirm which application is currently set up to open this file. The application icon here is actually a pull-down menu, which gives you a list of all the available programs on your Mac that could open this file. Just choose the one you prefer.

After you've changed the application to open the selected file, you might decide you want all files of this kind to be opened in this application. If so, simply click the Change All button at the bottom of the window to do this.

You can choose any compatible application to automatically open a document when you double-click on it, or even pick that application for all files of this kind.

Preview

This option is shown only when you select a document, and often enables you to see the contents of that document, whether it's text, an image, a video clip or a soundtrack. The Preview option may not work if Mac OS X is unable to properly analyse the file, though you can still open it with its parent application (or another application capable of handling that file type).

Privileges

This option enables you to choose which other users, sharing your Mac or on a local network, can see the selected file and in what ways they can change it. There's more on file privileges in the Guided Tour "Sharing Your Mac" on page 155.

Favorites

As you use your Mac over an extended period, there are certain folders you use again and again, whether it's saving a file to that location or visiting it in the Finder to open or change files. Some commonly-used locations are presented through the Finder toolbar and Go menu, but you can create your own list of Favorites, showing your preferred folders. You can also list files that you access often, such as documents or applications, but you may find that the Dock is a better area to store these. You can refer to your Favorites through the Finder toolbar, the Go menu or Open and Save dialogue boxes.

You can add a folder to your Favorites list by selecting it in the Finder and selecting **File > Add To Favorites**, or by clicking the "Add to Favorites" button in Open and Save dialogue boxes. You can remove Favorites by going to the Favorites folder through the Finder toolbar or Go menu, then dragging the surplus item from the Favorites folder into the Trash. This doesn't in any way affect the original file to which the Favorite refers.

V Applications in Mac OS X

You don't need to spend a fortune to start working with Mac OS X: it contains many applications for completing basic tasks, plus tools that can profoundly change your experience of the Mac.

17 Everyday Applications

Quick tip

For more assistance in using any of these applications, open the application and select **Help > Help**.

Installing an operating system isn't any fun if you don't get some new playthings to try out straight away. Fortunately, Mac OS X is brimming with applications that you can find on your hard disk after you've finished installing. In this chapter, we look briefly at all of Mac OS X's general programs, which you'll find in your Applications folder. In the next chapter, "Deep down and dirty", we reveal the applications that enable you to peek under Mac OS X's surface.

If you buy a new Mac, you may find other Mac OS X applications installed on your hard disk or supplied on CD-ROM, but the ones we look at here are the ones everyone gets as part of Mac OS X.

One of those little applications that comes in handy more often than you'd think, Calculator enables you to do a quick tot-up and even paste the result into a document.

Acrobat Reader

Acrobat Reader enables you to open PDF files,
documents that can be read by many different types
of computer. The documents can include images
and links, as well as a table of contents. Visit
www.adobe.com for more information.

Address Book

This contacts book stores names, phone numbers
and e-mail addresses as well as postal addresses. It
ties in closely with the Mail application, so that you
can add contacts to Address Book when you receive
an e-mail from them. The names and e-mails of
anyone you send a message to are automatically
added to Address Book.

Apple DVD Player

If your Mac has a DVD-ROM drive, you can insert
and watch video DVDs using this application.
Apple DVD Player opens when Mac OS X detects

You won't realise how
smart your Mac really is
until you take it on at
chess using the free
game included with
Mac OS X.

a video DVD and provides controls for playing, pausing and selecting DVD chapters.

Calculator

This application is a basic calculator with addition, subtraction, multiplication and division.

Quick tip

If your keyboard has a numeric keypad to its right, you can use this to type numbers into the Calculator: the keys on the pad correspond with the keys on the screen.

Clock

This application is a digital or analogue clock that you can have floating above all your other windows or showing the time in the Dock. It's a pretty alternative to the menu bar clock.

Image Capture

Quick tip

Image Capture transfers the images from a connected digital camera into your Pictures folder.

If you own a digital camera that includes a USB port, you may be able to connect it to your Mac, then use Image Capture to view the pictures stored in the camera and transfer your favourites onto your Mac's hard disk. Image Capture is compatible with dozens of digital camera models but isn't guaranteed to work with any given model.

iMovie

If you own a digital video camera with a FireWire port, you can connect it to your Mac and use iMovie to transfer footage over to your hard disk. You can

If you need a constant reminder of how far over your deadline you are, Clock has an insistent second hand that just keeps on ticking.

then edit the material, piecing clips together and adding special-effect transitions and titles. You can also add background music.

Internet Connect

This simple application enables you to open a modem-based Internet connection, giving you feedback on whether or not you're connected and how long you've been online for.

Internet Explorer

Browse the Web with the Mac OS X version of Microsoft's well-known Internet tool. You can see Web pages and add the ones you like to your list of Favorites to visit again later.

iTunes

Enjoy music and spoken-word material on your Mac with this MP3 and audio CD player. You can convert your favourite CDs into the digital MP3 format and make compilation discs by burning

Quick tip

Instead of Internet Connect, you can use the Connect option in the PPP Menu Extra to log on to the Internet. Each of these will generously confirm your connection if you use the other to connect.

Turn your Mac into a music centre with iTunes: you can convert your favourite CDs into digital tracks, which you can play on an MP3 player or make into a compilation CD.

tracks back onto CD (if you have a CD writer, either internally fitted in your Mac or external). You can also use your Internet connection to listen in on hundreds of Internet radio stations.

Mail

Check your e-mail with this application. You can log on to your various accounts to send and receive messages, which can include file attachments such as pictures.

Quick tip

For a small fee, you can upgrade QuickTime Player to enable you to play movies against a blank background and edit clips. Visit **www.apple.com/ quicktime** for details.

QuickTime Player

Play video clips in the well-known QuickTime and MPEG formats with this application. You can also use your Internet connection to tune into a selection of Net-based TV channels.

Whether it's the latest film trailer or your own home movie, you can enjoy digital video shown in pristine quality with QuickTime Player.

Preview

View image files and PDFs with this basic picture viewing application. You can save any document you open in Preview as a PDF file.

See also

Discover how Preview interacts with your printer in the Guided Tour "Go Go Gadget" on page 191.

Sherlock

Search your hard disk or the Internet with this powerful tool. With the hard disk search, you can look up file names or create an index of the contents of text documents in your Home, so that you can find out which document holds a word or phrase you're looking for. Sherlock's Internet search tools enable you to look up specific assets like contacts or products for sale, as well as looking through several famous search engines at once for general queries.

Quick tip

Activate Sherlock quickly while in the Finder with the keyboard shortcut Command-F.

Stickies

This basic text editor enables you to jot down memos and reminders on sheets that look just like the sticky notes you put on the fridge door.

System Preferences

Also available as an option in the Apple menu, this application enables you to customise the way Mac OS X behaves. We look extensively at System Preferences throughout this book, particularly in the Guided Tour "Your Personal Mac" on page 143.

TextEdit

Compose anything from a letter to a novel with this basic word processor. You can control the look of your document through Mac OS X's Font and Colors panels.

18 Deep Down and Dirty

As well as the general applications we looked at in the previous chapter, there's another kind that Mac OS X has plenty of: utilities that enable you to make changes to the way your Mac behaves and interacts with other devices. We've gathered these applications in their own chapter for one simple reason: this chapter carries a health warning for your Mac. Some of the programs here can do great things for your Mac but, in the wrong hands, they can cause a great deal of damage too. We'll advise you of the applications you should be wary of as we go through the list. Unless otherwise noted, you'll find these programs in **Applications/Utilities**.

AirPort Admin Utility

AirPort is Apple's system for linking Macs together by radio rather than physical cables. This tool

CPU Monitor presents a small window that shows you how busy your Mac is at the moment.

enables you to set up and maintain an AirPort
wireless network, giving you more control over
individual settings than AirPort Setup Assistant.

See also

Discover more about
AirPort in the Guided
Tour "Sharing Your
Mac" on page 155.

AirPort Setup Assistant

This is a basic tool for establishing a wireless network connection. Use AirPort Admin Utility for
more complicated setups than AirPort Setup
Assistant is able to cater for.

AppleScript

Use with caution. AppleScript is a built-in
programming language for Mac OS X that enables
to you script a series of actions for your Mac to take.
With AppleScript, you can write and save small
applications that trigger the actions you want; it's
like putting your Mac on auto-pilot. It's a powerful
and versatile technology that requires some study to
get the most out of it, but can be used to automate
pretty much anything. You'll find AppleScript tools
and some sample scripts to look through and try
in **Applications/AppleScript**.

See also

Visit **www.apple.com/
applescript** for more on
AppleScript, including
more sample scripts and
a free AppleScript Menu
Extra that enables you to
access scripts quickly.

Apple System Profiler

Ever wondered what's inside your Mac? This
application lays it all bare, displaying information
about the main hardware and operating system
components your Mac is using. You can look up
details like what external devices are plugged in
and where, or which System Extensions you have
installed. While's it's all of passing interest, System
Profiler's main role is in providing information to
help solve problems. If you ever call for technical
support and they start asking you questions about
your Mac, here is where you get the answers.

Applet Launcher

Java is a programming language for creating small applications or applets that can run on a variety of computers, including the Mac. Java applets can run from your hard disk (just double-click on them) or can be embedded in Web pages. You can go to the appropriate Web page in your Web browser, or type the Web address into Applet Launcher, which will run the applet without the help of a browser, just like a regular application.

ColorSync Utility

See also

There's more on ColorSync in the Guided Tour "Go Go Gadget" on page 191.

ColorSync is Apple's system for keeping colour in documents consistent, whether you're viewing them on your screen or printing them out. The system relies on "profiles" to describe each relevant device

Find out what makes your Mac tick with Apple System Profiler, which shows you everything from what processor you have to what's plugged into your Mac.

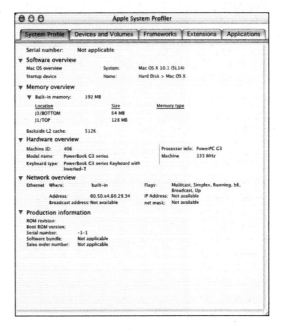

you use (printer, scanner, monitor, etc.). If you have problems getting accurate colour matches, this tool can check your profiles for errors.

Console

Like Apple System Profiler, this is predominantly a problem-solving tool, although you might find it interesting to take a look. Console simply shows detailed messages when Mac OS X has something to report, such as an error message. If your Mac is misbehaving, Console can help experienced Mac users work out what the cause could be.

CPU Monitor

Your Mac's processor has busy and quiet spells depending on the workload you give it. This tool enables you to see how busy your processor is at any moment with a simple meter, which you can display in its own window or in the Dock. You might be surprised at some of the processes that place the heaviest demands on your Mac.

DigitalColor Meter

This professional designer's tool enables you to target an area on your screen and find out how its colour is described in the formats commonly used in image editing applications like Photoshop. It's also a useful way to check that your screen's ColorSync profile is set up correctly.

Directory Setup

Use with caution. If your Mac is on a large network in an office or at college, you may be able to look up other people's address in a directory stored elsewhere on the network. This utility helps you change the location that your Mac refers to when searching for a contact, so it's best left to technical support teams who know where to point it.

Disk Copy

Quick tip

If you receive a file with the filename extension .dmg, it's typically a disk image. Double-click on the file to make Disk Copy open it up and display its contents.

Some files, particularly applications ready for installation onto your Mac, are packaged up as disk images, essentially wrappers for pretend hard disks. Disk Copy open ups the disk image; you can then open a window to show its contents and copy files onto your hard disk.

Disk Utility

Use with great caution. If you want to erase a hard disk or a removable media volume, start up Disk Utility. You'll see a list of storage volumes currently in use by your Mac; click on the appropriate icon and you can erase the disk. Always double-check you have selected the correct disk before you erase it: there's no going back afterwards. Disk Utility is able to erase hard disks, floppy disks, Iomega Zip disks, Imation SuperDisks and rewritable CDs. The application provides several other options,

Disk Utility enables you to check, repair and customise storage volumes of all kinds – you can even erase a CD-RW so it's ready to use again.

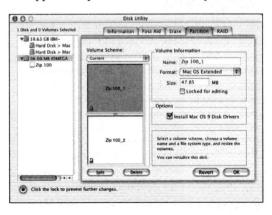

including the ability to check and repair the surface of disks if you believe they're damaged, or to partition disks into more than one independent section. Anything you do in Disk Utility has the potential to erase important files, so be careful.

Display Calibrator

ColorSync is Apple's system for keeping colour in documents consistent, whether you're viewing them on your screen or printing them out. This tool creates a profile for your screen to match against other devices, such as scanners and printers.

Grab

This tool captures almost anything you can see on your screen for posterity, saving the image as a file on your Desktop. You can capture the entire screen or just a selected part of it. Mac OS X also offers keyboard shortcuts to take immediate screen grabs. Press Command-Shift-3 to capture an image of the entire screen. Press Command-Shift-4 to capture a selected area. As soon as you hit this key combination, your cursor turns into a cross-hair. Move the cursor to the top-left of the area you want to capture, then click and hold while moving to the bottom-right of the capture area. Release the mouse button to capture the area you've marked out.

Installer

Many of the new applications you receive are packaged as installer files that you simply double-click to activate. It's a good system because you can be sure that no components you need to run the software are missing. Installer helps this process along, and you will probably never have to double-click on the application itself.

Java Web Start

Java is a programming language for creating small applications or applets that can run on a variety of computers, including the Mac. Java Web Start is a tool for managing Java applications that you can download from the Internet and run on your Mac: it ensures that you always have the latest version of any Java application and provides a list of the applications you've already downloaded.

Key Caps

Quick tip

Always choose the font you're using at the time in Key Caps, so you can be sure the feedback given is correct. Being able to switch fonts in Key Caps is also handy to find out how to get the character you want in symbol or pictographic fonts like Zapf Dingbats.

It isn't always obvious which key or combination of keys you need to press in order to enter a character into your document. How do you get an acute accent over a letter, for example? Key Caps gives you a visual representation of your own keyboard, so that you can hold down modifier keys like Shift and Option and see in advance what the result will be. Hold down Option, for example, and you'll see that Option-E gives you an acute accent (you then type the letter you want the accent over, such as e or a – if you type a letter that the selected accent can't appear over, nothing appears).

Keychain Access

If you have passwords or other details you want to keep private, store them in Keychain Access. A Keychain is simply a document holding a description and other details of your private information. Keychains are often used to store Website passwords and e-mail access codes, but you could put in credit card numbers or National Insurance details, for example – anything you might need to look up but want to keep secret. Your master password unlocks the whole Keychain.

NetInfo Manager

Use with caution. If your Mac is connected to a network, Mac OS X uses its NetInfo system to keep track of which computers and users are linked. NetInfo Manager enables anyone setting up a large, complicated network to control precisely how it operates. Most people should never need to run the program, and tampering with its settings could affect your existing connections.

Network Utility

Here's another problem-solving tool that technical support teams will appreciate but you might find life is too short for: this one provides feedback on how your network connection is operating. You can check details like IP addresses, for example.

Print Center

Once you've connected a printer to your Mac, you must register its presence before you can use it. The

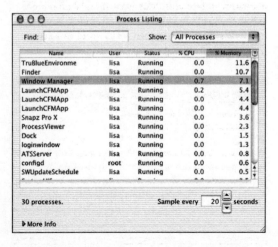

Find out exactly what your Mac is doing right now with Process Viewer, which lists every function running in Mac OS X.

process will happen automatically for many printer models; for the rest, there's Print Center. Use this to make your Mac look for printers through a specific port, such as USB or Ethernet. You'll get a list of connected printers; choose the one you want to use.

See also

There's more on printing in the Guided Tour "Go Go Gadget" on page 191.

Process Viewer

Use with caution. Mac OS X and its applications rely on "processes", which are basically consistent threads of specific actions that the Mac has to carry out in order to maintain whatever you're doing. The operating system itself runs several processes at once, while individual applications can refer to other processes and are usually represented by a process themselves. Process Viewer enables you to look in on what your Mac is doing right now. It shows a list of all active processes, which you can list in order of the amount of processor time they're using or the amount of memory they occupy. These figures change constantly, so you can set Process Viewer to update the list every few seconds. You can also make a process quit, which is where you should use some caution; it shouldn't ever be necessary unless your Mac is badly misbehaving. While the list is mostly of use to technical support teams, it's interesting to see which applications are hogging your Mac's time.

Network Utility provides penetrating access to the deeper recesses of your Mac network and Internet connection – dead useful if you can understand any of it.

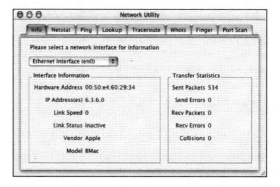

StuffIt Expander

Many of the files you receive on your Mac, especially those you download from the Internet, are compressed into a single archive to save space. StuffIt Expander, as the name suggests, decompresses these (it can deal with all the most common archive formats you'll encounter) so that you can access the files within.

Quick tip

StuffIt Expander can open correctly-made archives with the filename extensions .bin, .cpt, .gz, .hqx, .sit, .tar or .zip.

Terminal

Use with great caution. As we discover in the Guided Tour "How Mac OS X Works" on page 215, Mac OS X is driven by an extremely powerful core operating system called Unix. Unix itself is decades old, hailing from a time before Macs or Microsoft Windows. In those days, you had to type every instruction into your computer, and any feedback you got was also presented only as text – no images, no variety of fonts. While computer technology has clearly moved on, many people with extensive computing experience and technically demanding jobs still prefer the old method – what's called a command line interface. CLIs are difficult to learn and demand concentration to use, but can give you far more extensive control over a computer than a standard graphical interface, because they can do things that nobody would take the trouble to create a graphical interface for.

Quick tip

If you feel brave and want to start exploring what Terminal can do, start at the Website **www.freebsd.org**, which offers advice for newcomers and experts alike. Make sure you back up your entire hard disk before you start using Terminal.

Terminal is the CLI application for Mac OS X, allowing access to the heart of the operating system. It enables people with in-depth knowledge of Unix to customise the Mac for difficult tasks like hosting Web sites. If you don't know what you're doing, though, you can easily type in the wrong thing and ruin essential system files. Terminal is simultaneously the most powerful and the most dangerous application on your hard disk.

VI Guided Tours

Take a tour round an everyday area of
Mac activity, and discover how Mac OS X
can help. Explore customising your Mac,
sharing your Mac with others, going online,
connecting external devices, working with
Mac OS 9, and using fonts, then discover
how Mac OS X actually works beneath
the surface.

19 Your Personal Mac

One of the best things about using Mac OS X is that it enables you to tailor the operating system's look and behaviour to suit yourself. The heart of this flexibility is System Preferences, which you can find in the Applications folder or in the Apple menu – it's also in the Dock by default when you use Mac OS X after installation. The System Preferences window is divided into four themed sections, enabling you to configure your Mac in many different ways. Just click on the appropriate icon to switch to the controls you need. Most of these

Open the System Preferences application for a feast of options that help your Mac work more effectively and behave just the way you want it to.

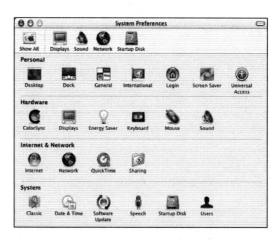

controls affect only your use of the Mac; other people logging into their own user accounts can choose their own preferences. Some areas affect everyone, however, so they can be locked by anyone with Administrator privileges to prevent others from tinkering with the settings.

Personal

This group of controls directly affects how your Mac looks and behaves.

Desktop

Use this control to change the picture used on your Desktop. Choose an image from the collections offered in the pull-down menu, or pick one of your own images from your Pictures folder. You can also drag an image file of your choice into the well area labelled in this window.

Dock

This control adjusts the Dock that stores shortcuts to your favourite applications and other files. You can adjust the size of the Dock itself or the extent to which it magnifies icons as you pass your mouse over them. Untick the Magnification checkbox if

Quick tip

The toolbar in System Preferences is always available and holds the controls you use most often. To remove a control, drag its icon from the toolbar. To add a control, click on Show All, then drag the icon you want into the toolbar. You can also drag icons around within the toolbar to change their positions.

Quick tip

The best images to use as a Desktop picture are those that are in the same resolution that your screen is set to, or perhaps higher. The picture should ideally also be in proportion to your screen.

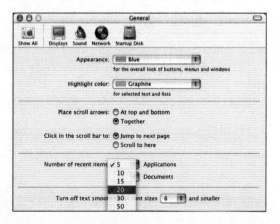

The General area holds a disparate set of options for making your Mac look and behave differently.

Quick tip

Many of these controls
are available under
Apple > Dock or
directly in the Dock
itself. Hold down the
Control key and click
on the Dock's divider
line to see the options.

you don't want to use the latter feature. You can
also decide whether you want to position the Dock
along the bottom of the screen or to either the left
or right side. You can then choose to have the Dock
hidden out of sight, off the edge of the screen.
When ou move your mouse to that edge, the Dock
emerges to give you access to its contents, sliding
back out of view once you select the icon you want.

There are two further options connected with
animating Dock actions. When you minimise a
window using its yellow window button, Mac OS X
applies a special effect as the window shrinks down
into the Dock. Choose here which effect you prefer
– "Scale" is quicker than "Genie". Finally, you can
choose to animate icons when you start an
application. This will make the icon bounce up and
down while the application is launching; when it
settles again, the application is ready to use.

General
A loosely connected set of controls that Apple
probably couldn't find a better name for... Here you
can change the overall colour scheme you're using
or the colour used to highlight selections, perhaps

Mac OS X can work
in many different
languages; the
International area is
where you control which
language you use, and
how local niceties like
date formats are shown.

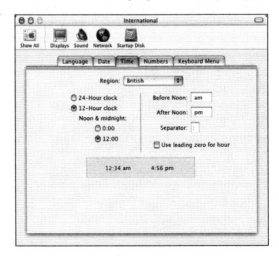

to complement the image you use as your Desktop picture. You can also decide whether to place scroll arrows at each end of a scroll bar to group them together, as well as decide what action is triggered by clicking in the scroll bar itself.

Next, you can choose how many items should be remembered in the list of applications and documents you last used, which you look up under **Recent Items** in the Apple menu. Finally, you can decide which type size should see text smoothing turned off on your screen. Mac OS X smoothes out the fonts it displays, but some people feel that text then becomes fuzzy and indistinct at smaller sizes.

International

This control affects how different languages are used and presented on your Mac. The Language tab dictates the order in which languages are used in Mac OS X menus and other controls. If a control label isn't available in your preferred language, Mac OS X will attempt to show it in the next language in the list. This area also affects scripts, which are broad behaviour guidelines for different kinds of alphabets. Most Western languages are based on the Roman script, for example. Within this, there may be different behaviours for your own language. All of this will have been decided for you when you

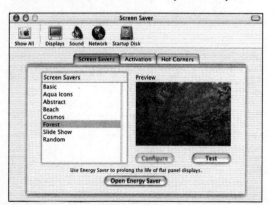

You may not really need to run it, but the Screen Saver is an attractive way of showing when your Mac is taking a break.

told Mac OS X which language you wanted to use during installation, but you can change behaviours here. Not too important if you use only English!

The Date, Time and Numbers tabs affect how these kinds of information are presented on your Mac. (The Numbers tab also affects currency.) Click on the relevant tab to choose the region that best reflects your own preferences, or make the changes yourself in the fields provided. (The region name will then change to "Custom".)

The Keyboard Menu tab enables you to choose which regions should be listed in the Keyboard menu. If you tick one checkbox only, the Keyboard menu isn't visible and only the one keyboard layout is available. Tick another checkbox and the menu appears, enabling you to switch regions easily.

Login

This control affects how you log in when you start using your Mac and helps you start applications automatically upon login if you wish. The Login Window tab enables you to change the look and behaviour of the Login process, which we look at in the Guided Tour "Sharing Your Mac" on page 155.

If a disability means you have difficulty using the mouse or keyboard shortcuts, Universal Access can make these tasks more comfortable – also good for beginners.

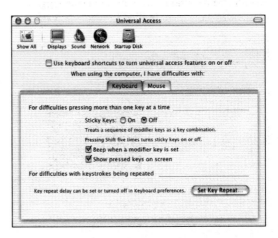

The Login Items tab enables you to choose items that will start automatically each time you log in. These will typically be applications you use throughout a session, such as Mail, but you can also pick documents to open on login, such as a word processing document you're working on a great deal. To add an item to the list, click the Add button and select the application in the dialogue box that appears. Once an item is in the list, tick its checkbox if you want it hidden from view while it starts up – you can switch to that item later by clicking its icon in the Dock. Change the order in which items are activated by dragging them to elsewhere in the list. To remove an item from the list, click on it to highlight it and click the Remove button.

Screen Saver

Screen savers are animations that take over your Mac when it hasn't been used for a set time. The original idea was to protect your screen from harm when you leave your Mac switched on for long periods without using it. There was once a fear of screen images getting "burned" into the display permanently, but modern screen technologies mean the risk is insignificant – screen savers nowadays are mainly just for fun. That said, though, they can

Quick tip

Administrators can lock the Login Window tab to prevent others from changing the settings. This does not affect your access to the Login Items tab.

Mac upgraders

Login Items replaces the previous Startup Items system with a system more suited to multiple users.

Change your monitor resolution in the Displays area – although you may regret the idea if you use a flat-screen LCD monitor.

Quick tip

You can download
more screen savers
and install them on your
Mac. Look for them in
the Downloads section
at **www.apple.com/
macosx**. Copy the files
after download into
Library/Screen Savers
for every user to enjoy;
to keep the new screen
saver to yourself, create
a folder called Screen
Savers in **~/Library** and
copy the files there.

Quick tip

If you have difficulty
using the mouse, you
can also immediately
access key features like
menus and the Dock
using the keyboard. See
the section about Key-
board control later in this
chapter to find out how
to set up access.

It never hurts to
conserve energy,
especially if you use a
laptop. the Energy Saver
area gives you control
over when your Mac
starts to wind down.

be used as a security feature to blank your screen if
you're away from your Mac for any length of time,
and can be set to require a password before your
screen is activated again. This control enables you to
choose a screen saver to view, as well as setting the
period of time that should pass before it activates.

Universal Access
This control aims to help some people who have
physical difficulty using a Mac, perhaps because of
a disability. If you find it difficult to use the
keyboard shortcuts we describe throughout the
book, which rely on holding down two or more
keys at once, turn on Sticky Keys through the
Keyboard tab. This enables you to press each
modifier key you need one at a time, rather than
holding it down while you press the next key. The
character you type will appear on the screen.

The controls under the Mouse tab enable you to
move the mouse cursor using the numeric keypad
on your keyboard.

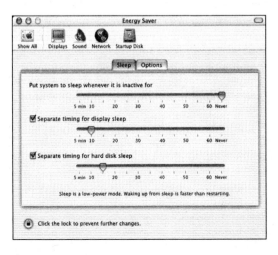

Hardware

This group of controls affects how your Mac interacts with other devices.

ColorSync

ColorSync is Apple's technology for matching colours as they appear on your screen and through other devices, such as scanners and printers. This control affects which profiles are picked automatically when you haven't already chosen one for a specific situation.

See also

See the Guided Tour "Go Go Gadget" on page 191 for more on ColorSync.

Displays

This control changes the resolution in which your screen is presenting information. The list here can show all options available or only the ones recommended for your monitor. Note that some flat-screen displays are designed to be used only at one resolution, and the quality of your screen image may be affected if you change resolution. You can also change the screen brightness and the number of colours it's using (i.e., how many steps it slices the spectrum into; more steps can be invaluable for

Extra help for anyone who finds it hard to use a mouse: use the Keyboard area to access the menu bar and Dock through your keyboard.

distinguishing colours accurately), as well as
picking its ColorSync profile.

Energy Saver

Quick tip

Administrators can lock
the Energy Saver
controls to prevent
others changing them.

Macs are highly energy-efficient, but this control
helps you save even more power – especially useful
if you have a laptop and are running it on its
batteries. With the Sleep tab, you can set a time after
which the Mac will go to sleep, or set separate time
limits for the hard disk to wind down or for the
display to dim, without the Mac going to sleep.

Keyboard

Quick tip

If you have a laptop, the
Mouse control will adjust
your trackpad speed. If
you plug a mouse into
your laptop's USB port,
you will see tabs for both
control devices so you
can make separate
adjustments to each.

The Repeat Rate tab adjusts your keyboard's
responsiveness to your touch, while Full Keyboard
Access enables you to set up controls to replace the
mouse if you have difficulty using it. Once access is
enabled using the checkbox "Turn on full keyboard
access", you can navigate the menu bar and the
Dock, plus window toolbars and application
palettes, using only the keyboard. The control here
sets the keys that trigger keyboard access; you then
use the arrow keys to move between items, and the
Return key to activate an item once it's selected.

If you use a laptop with
a mouse plugged in as
well, the Mouse area
splits into two to give
you precise control over
both your mouse and
your trackpad.

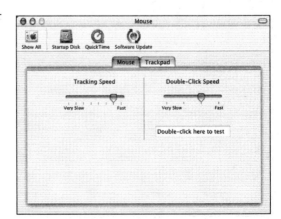

Mouse

This control adjusts the speed and responsiveness of your mouse or other control device.

Sound

This control adjusts your Mac's volume and enables you to choose the alert sound you prefer.

Internet & Network

This group holds the settings that enable your Mac to connect to the Internet.

Internet

This control stores settings that can be applied across many Internet programs on your Mac. Many people use than one Web browser, for example, so the settings stored here can be applied to all the Web browsers on your Mac.

Network

This area stores all the settings you need to establish a connection with local networks and the Internet. It includes facilities to switch between different

See also

Explore all the Internet & Network controls in more detail as part of the Guided Tour "Mac OS X Online" on page 169.

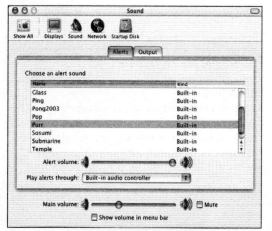

Open up the Sounds area to choose the sound your Mac makes when it needs to get your attention. It's great fun experimenting with the noises in the list.

Quick tip

Administrators can lock
the Network controls to
prevent other users
changing them.

groups of settings – for example, between different
Internet service providers, if you have accounts
with more than one, or between an office network
and your home setup, if you use your portable in
more than one location.

QuickTime

QuickTime is Apple's technology for playing video
clips and other digital media. This control affects
how QuickTime treats material received over the
Internet, and gives access to some related settings.

Sharing

Quick tip

Administrators can lock
the Sharing controls to
prevent other users
changing them.

The Sharing area enables other Macs to connect
with yours, both through local networks and the
Internet. You can also offer Web pages for others to
read over a network. There's coverage of the
Sharing Controls in two later Guided Tours: "Mac
OS X online" and "Sharing Your Mac".

System

This group affects some of the operating system's
most fundamental settings.

Classic

The Classic panel controls your use of the Classic
environment, which OS X uses to run applications
written for older versions of the Mac OS. See the
Guided Tour "Living with the Legacy" on page 201.

Date & Time

Quick tip

Administrators can lock
the Date & Time controls
to prevent other users
changing them.

This control enables you to change the time used by
your Mac. You can set the date, time and the region
of the world in which you live. You should already
have applied the correct settings for these as part of
the installation process. You can also choose a server
to relay an accurate time over the Internet, and
change the appearance of the menu bar clock.

Software Update
As Apple releases minor revisions to Mac OS X,
Software Update is able to find them on the
Internet, then download and install them.

Speech
This control enables you to speak selected
commands into your Mac (assuming you have a
microphone connected, of course), and to listen to
text being read out by it. You can select the voice it
uses to read text out by clicking on the Text-to-
Speech tab and choosing from the list.

Startup Disk
Use this control to exit Mac OS X and start up in
Mac OS 9. See how Startup Disk enables you to
interact with Mac OS 9 in the Guided Tour
"Living with the Legacy" on page 201.

Users
The Users control enables you to create new user
accounts or to change the behaviour of existing
accounts. Get to know your fellow users in the
next Guided Tour, "Sharing Your Mac".

See also

Explore Software Update
further in the Guided
Tour "Mac OS X Online"
on page 169.

Quick tip

Not all applications
support Text-to-Speech;
look for an option like
TextEdit's "Speech" (in
its Edit menu). There
seems to be a bug in
TextEdit's current
implementation of it,
though: "Stop Speaking"
is always unavailable!

Quick tip

Administrators can lock
the Startup Disk and the
Users controls to prevent
others changing them.

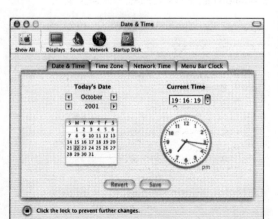

Make sure your clock is
spot-on with the Date &
Time controls; you can
also change the way the
menu bar clock looks
here.

20 Sharing Your Mac

Communication has become as central to computers as their original role of processing information. Mac OS X is designed to further communication in two ways: among several people using the same Mac, and among several Macs and other computers linked through a private network.

One Mac, several people

You might share access to the Mac you use with several others; the most common instance, of

If you are the only person to use your Mac, you can change the Login preferences so that your account logs in automatically each time you start your Mac.

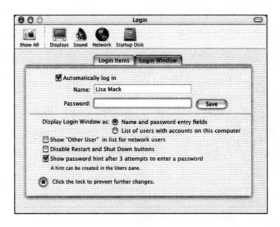

course, is when a family or household shares one Mac between them. The backbone of this option is Mac OS X's deployment of separate areas for each individual, a concept that runs through the fabric of the entire operating system. Each person who has access to Mac OS X is invited to create a user account, which maintains the documents they work on and their choices of how Mac OS X should be set up. (Some users might have limitations on what settings they can alter, though – see the section on "Access privileges" below.)

Every Mac running Mac OS X has to have at least one user account before it will work. Beyond that, you're not obliged to add further accounts, but making accounts for different people lets everyone enjoy a measure of privacy and the ability to customise their experience of the Mac. Each registered user has their own "Home" folder, which stores their documents and individual preferences. When a user opens the Mail application, for example, the program refers to their Home to present the e-mail messages stored there. Internet Explorer takes its Favorites list of regularly-visited Websites from the Home of the user opening the browser. The system also protects your documents from others sharing access to the Mac, unless you opt to make files available.

These are the key concepts that will help you share your Mac effectively:

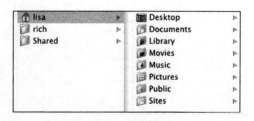

When Lisa is logged on, she can see her own Home folders and access any file inside them.

Quick tip

If you are the only person to use your Mac, you can choose to bypass the Login process. Open System Preferences and click Login, then select the Login Window tab. Tick the checkbox next to "Automatically log in" and enter the user name and password that should be entered when your Mac starts up.

Account login

Each user is able to open their own settings and access their own documents in Mac OS X. To do this, you first need to log into your own user account. When Mac OS X starts up, it reaches a point where it asks you for a user name and password; that person is then logged in, and the Mac will appear in the state they left it the last time they used it. Once you're logged in, you can run any program in the main Applications folder or customise the way Mac OS X looks and behaves while you're using it.

If you share your Mac with others, you should always log out when you have finished what you are doing – you may not be the next person to use the Mac. Logging out gives you a chance to save any open documents, then closes all active applications before displaying the Login window for the next person.

Any Administrator can customise the look of the Login window and the options users have. One Login design presents a list of every user who has an account on the Mac; to log in, click the relevant user name, then enter your password. The other design simply presents blank text fields into which you enter your user name and password. To select the design that appears, open System Preferences and click Login, then select the Login Window tab to access the choice of designs.

Lisa's personal folders in her Home are protected from view when other people are logged on, although she can leave files to collect in her Public folder.

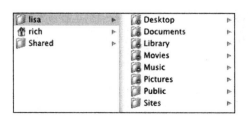

Access privileges

Some users have the ability to alter every setting in
Mac OS X, while others have restricted access. The
more senior users are known as Administrators:
they are able to make changes that may affect other
users as well as themselves, such as installing or
removing software. Changes to the Mac setup that
affect the entire Mac, rather than just the user who's
logged in, can be protected so that you have to enter
an Administrator-level user name and password
before you can change anything. Areas that may be
protected include updates for Mac OS X itself, some
software installations and some System Preferences
areas. (We noted some in the previous chapter.)

The first user account to be created, during the
initial Mac OS X installation process, is always
at Administrator level, and that status cannot be
changed. This Administrator is able to create further
accounts, and decide the level of access that each
account should enjoy. Within a family, for example,
the parents might each have an Administrator-level
account, while the kids are given a standard or
User-level account. This will let them change their
own Desktop picture or decide what applications
should be shown in their Dock, but will prevent
them from removing items that everyone else needs.
(In some households, of course, the kids should
have control while the computer dunce parents are
prevented from damaging anything.) This privilege
system can also be used in a workplace to stop
employees changing important Mac settings, so that
the tech support team isn't tied up by firefighting
preventable issues.

Adding and removing users

Anyone with Administrator-level access can
introduce additional users to the roster on your
Mac. The lineup is managed in the Users area
within System Preferences. When you add a user,
you must give them a name, in both long and short
formats, which are displayed at different times as

Quick tip

If you're unable to
access controls in a
System Preferences
area or application
installer, look for a lock
icon to click on. You'll
then be asked for an
Administrator-level user
name and password.

you use your Mac. The short-format name is given to the Home folder in which that user will store their documents. You must also enter a password, and have the option of providing a hint in case the password is forgotten. Finally, you must decide whether or not the new user should have Administrator-level privileges.

Quick tip

Removing a user moves all their documents into the folder belonging to the Administrator responsible, so that none of the user's files are lost unintentionally. All that user's preferences are deleted, though.

As well as adding or removing users, you can make changes to individual accounts. You can change a user's long-format name, but not their short-format name. You can also change the password or the password hint, as well as their Administrator status. You cannot change the status of the first user account to be created, although you can remove that user once there's another Administrator.

Networked Macs

Instead of several people sharing the Mac you use (or in addition to that), you may be in a situation where your Mac is linked to other Macs or PCs. A local network like this can include several

When you create a new user account in System Preferences, you can decide which folders they can access and which login picture they can have.

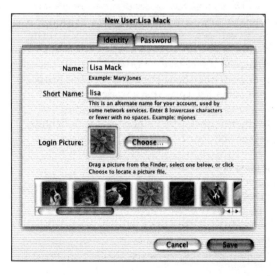

hundred computers or just two. After acting as the backbone of many offices for years, networks on a smaller scale are becoming more and more common at home, as households build a collection of two or more computers.

The most common way to link up various computers is through physical cables. Ethernet is the de facto standard system that specifies the shape of the cable sockets and how the data is passed between machines. An increasingly popular alternative, especially in homes where installing loads of cabling isn't a feasible option, is wireless networking, where the data is passed over radio waves. Apple's AirPort technology, an option in all current Macs, is a wireless network system based on the IEEE 802.11 industry specification, which means that Macs can connect wirelessly with other computers using the same standard.

There's a central relationship between computers in any network, large or small: the relationship between client and server. A server is a computer given the task of storing material for other computers to access; a client is any computer that connects to the server to obtain that material. In a small network, like the one in a home, you might choose the main machine to act as the server, even though it will be used for other tasks too. In the larger networks typically found in offices, some computers act only as servers, existing purely to serve up files for visiting clients. The same relationship is in effect when you use the Internet, by the way: your Mac is a client linking to a server elsewhere on the Net, which might store Web pages or e-mail messages, for instance.

The busiest networks, with perhaps hundreds of users connected, will use specialist software to cope with the heavy demand. One such option is Mac OS X Server, the variation of Mac OS X we mentioned in the earlier chapter "Meet the Mac". Mac OS X

Server is designed specifically to deliver files and other content over networks as efficiently as possible, rather than run general applications as most Macs do.

Activating your network

There are two key network protocols through which you can link your Mac to other computers. (Think of a protocol as a language that all the computers on the network agree to talk for the sake of sharing information, regardless of how they're connected or what the "native" language of each might be.) AppleTalk is a networking system designed specifically for Mac-only environments, making it ideal for home use as well as in Mac-based offices. It's easy to set up: just give every Mac in the network a different name in its Sharing area within System Preferences.

TCP/IP is the system the Internet uses to move information from machine to machine, but it can work equally well over local networks. It's more complicated to set up than AppleTalk, but makes it easier to have Macs and PCs sharing the same

In the Sharing area of System Preferences, you can choose the Mac name others see when they access your Mac through a network.

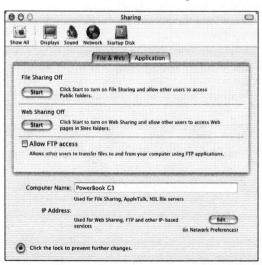

network. Under TCP/IP, every computer in the
network has its own identity code or IP address,
stored as a sequence of four groups of numbers
separated by full-stops (periods) – for example,
123.45.67.89 or 1.2.3.4 (the number in each group
may range between 0 and 999, but there must be
four groups).

The IP address system is most commonly found
on the Internet, where every computer has its own
numerical sequence. When you type in a Website
address, for example, that address is tied in with an
IP address that your computer uses to find the Web
server that's storing the pages you want. (It does
this by querying a dedicated Domain Name Server,
which lists Website addresses and the IP numbers
that correspond with each.)

Within a local network, each computer using
TCP/IP also must have its own IP address. If your
Mac is part of an office network, it will probably
already have an IP address, enabling others to find
your Mac on the network if necessary or to give you
access to the Internet via your company server. If
you're setting up a network yourself, you must
choose unique IP addresses for each machine that's
connected to it, either entering the address into each
Mac manually or using a DHCP server to distribute
the addresses automatically.

Whether you're using AppleTalk or TCP/IP for
your network, you must decide which Macs are
to act as servers, which the rest automatically
nominated as clients. If there are only a few Macs
to link together, it's likely that any Mac acting as a
server will also be used to run applications. You
must first give each Mac its own identity; do this
for every Mac, whether they're going to function
as clients or servers.

To link via **AppleTalk**, go to the Sharing pane in
System Preferences and, under Network Identity,

See also

Some IP addresses are
reserved for particular
uses – see "Mac OS X
Online" on page 169.

type a name into the Computer Name field. Then
go to the Network area and select the means by
which your Mac will be connected – either Ethernet
or AirPort. Click on the AppleTalk tab and tick the
Make AppleTalk Active box. Click the Save button
to complete the task and activate AppleTalk. The
AppleTalk Zone option shown here is for use in
larger office networks, which might use several
servers to cater for different areas or buildings.
When you activate AppleTalk, the available zone
names will be displayed here, and your technical
support team will inform you which zone you
should have. You won't have to bother with zones
if you're setting up a small network.

If you're going to link via **TCP/IP**, go to the
Network area in System Preferences and select
the means by which your Mac will be connected –
either Ethernet or AirPort. Click on the TCP/IP tab.
From the Configure pull-down menu, choose
Manually, then enter the appropriate sequence in
the IP Address field. If you're using a reserved IP
address such 10.0.0.1, this won't interfere with the

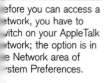

efore you can access a
twork, you have to
vitch on your AppleTalk
twork; the option is in
e Network area of
stem Preferences.

TCP/IP settings you already have entered to access the Internet through your modem.

Once you've set up every Mac, you can activate your server or servers. For each server, go to the Sharing pane in System Preferences, where you'll see a section headed File Sharing Off. Click on the Start button here to activate sharing. This may take a few moments, after which the message above the button will change to File Sharing On. This makes the Mac visible to others over the network.

Connecting to a server

Once your network is active, you're ready to connect to any servers on it. Use the Finder to locate the server you need: choose **Go > Connect To Server** to see a list of available servers. You can also just type in the AppleTalk name or IP address (as appropriate) of the server you want. Mac OS X is able to recognise all the major network connection protocols used in office environments, including NFS and Samba.

Once you are connected to a server, its behaviour on your Mac is the same as a storage volume, such as a hard disk or removable storage medium. The server's icon appears in the Finder; to view it, choose **Go > Computer**, where you'll see it alongside your hard disk and other volumes. To disconnect from the server, select its icon in the Finder, then choose **File > Eject**.

Sharing files

Mac OS X provides four ways to make files available to other users, which may apply to users sharing your Mac or to those connected to you via a network. If you want to make material available over a network, you must activate File Sharing.

Quick tip

If there's a server you access frequently, use the Add to Favorites button to include that server in the pull-down menu within the Connect To Server dialogue box.

Quick tip

It's a good idea to disconnect from a server as soon as you've finished using it, rather than keeping it there permanently. If the server has technical problems or is shut down for any reason, this can affect your Mac too.

Quick tip

If your Mac has File Sharing switched on, others on the network can see your Public folder and Drop Box. If you have several users set up on the Mac, all their Public folders will be accessible in this way, so make sure they know this.

Quick tip

If you regularly pass documents on to another user, create an Alias of their Drop Box and leave it on your Desktop, or drag their Drop Box icon into your Dock or Finder Toolbar to create a handy shortcut to it.

The Public folder

This is the link between you and other Mac users, whether they're sharing the same Mac or are linked to yours via a network. Other users are not able to view the contents of the rest of your Home, but they can visit this folder to collect any file you leave here, or to deposit a file they want you to see. To make a file available for others to see or transfer to their computer, copy it into the Public folder. You can also create sub-folders inside the Public folder if you choose.

Placed within the Public folder, the Drop Box is the folder others can use to leave files on your Mac. To access another user's Drop Box on your Mac, open that person's Home folder, then the Public folder inside that. You'll see the Drop Box there, enabling you to copy files into it.

The Shared folder

Based in the Users folder, which also stores each user's Home, the Shared folder is a general area available to everyone who shares your Mac. It's useful for leaving documents that more than person is working on at different times, for example.

Control exactly who can open or change one of your documents by altering its file privileges.

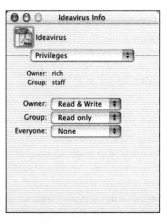

The Network volume

Based in the Computer area, the level that shows
all your storage volumes, Network is like a Shared
folder that's available across an entire network. It's
designed for Macs that are acting predominantly
as servers, enabling them to make applications,
documents or other items such as fonts available
to every user logged on to that server. To make an
item available, move it to the Network volume on
your Mac, where you'll find standard folders such
as Applications, Library and Users.

Web sharing

Mac OS X can host Web pages or entire sites that
others can access over a network or while sharing
your Mac. If you place HTML documents you have
created in your Home's Sites folder, others can view
those pages through their Web browser at the
address **http://computername/~username/** –
where the computername is whatever you've
called your Mac in the Sharing pane in System
Preferences; the username is the shorter of the two
names you chose for your Home. You'll need to tell
users the names of all the HTML documents you
want them to see, so they can add the name of each
page at the end of this address; or you can create a
main page within your Home's Sites folder called
index.html, which will be visible automatically as
soon as visitors access that address and help them
to find the other pages.

Web sharing is not really designed for use over the
Internet, only local networks or within a shared
Mac setup. Your Internet connection is unlikely to
be fast enough to cope with the demands of many
people connecting at once or to be available 24
hours a day, so hosting Web pages for Internet
access is best left to powerful specialised servers.
To activate Web Sharing, open the Sharing area in
System Preferences, where you'll see a section
headed Web Sharing Off. Click the Start button
below to activate.

Quick tip

You can create HTML
documents with word
processors like Apple-
Works or Microsoft
Word, or professional
graphical Web publishing
packages such as Adobe
GoLive or Macromedia
Dreamweaver. For
details of how to go
about it, consult your
preferred application's
manuals or user guides.

File privileges

You can precisely control exactly who has access
to the files you leave in any of the sharing areas
described above. If you work in a large company,
for example, you might want to make a document
available to others in your team, but not to anyone
else in the firm. That's why every file and folder
available in Mac OS X has a set of privileges
assigned to it, dictating who can access that file or
folder and what they're permitted to do with it.
To change a file or folder's privileges, select the
item in the Finder, then select **File > Show Info** and
choose Privileges from the Show Info window's
pull-down menu.

uick tip

you change a folder's
vileges and you want
ur new setting
flected in other folders
side that one, click the
ply button below the
ll-down menus.

Here you can see who the "owner" of the item is,
and which group they belong to. Groups are
collections of people with some kind of association.
Usually Mac OS X assigns the group name for each
user on the Mac automatically, and every user on
your Mac belongs to the same group, "staff". Some
items, notably applications, belong to the "admin"
group, which means only users with Administrator
privileges can change those files; other items, such
as files in the System folder, belong to the group
"wheel", which prevents anyone from changing the
file. If you need manual control over group names,
because you are creating a large network in an
office, for example, you can create groups and
assign users in NetInfo Manager.

There are also three pull-down menus that enable
you to change the privileges for different categories
of user: the item owner, the group to which the
owner belongs, and everyone else with access to
your Mac over a network. You can change each of
these so that a user category can only read a item,
only write a item, do both or do neither.

As an example, select your own Home's Public
folder and select **File > Show Info,** then choose

Privileges from the pull-down menu. You can see your own name as the owner and "staff" as the group name. As the owner, you have Read & Write privileges in this folder, so you can add or remove files at will. The rest of the group, and others connecting via a network, have Read Only privileges, which means they can see the folder's contents and open documents, but they cannot change them. If you look at the privileges of the Drop Box inside your Public folder, you can see that groups and everyone else now have Write Only privileges, so they can copy files into the Drop Box for you, but can't open or remove any files already in there.

Quick tip

If the pull-down menus under Privileges are faded out, it means you do not have the necessary permission to alter this file. Try logging out and then logging in again as a user with Administrator privileges.

21 Mac OS X Online

Because Mac OS X has been designed since the Internet explosion, it exploits the ability to go online further than perhaps any previous operating system. Without the help of any software beyond what's provided when you install, Mac OS X enables you to: browse the Web and download files; discover new applications available for Mac OS X; update your operating system software; send and receive e-mail; get up-to-the-minute assistance; make sure your Mac's clock is 100% accurate; quickly present a Website or make a simple home page; watch TV and listen to radio broadcast over the Net; and share files with friends and colleagues. With extra software, you can also protect your Mac against predatory hackers on the Net. But before you do any of that, of course, you need a working Internet connection.

Connection options

There are several ways to connect your Mac to the Internet:

Standard dialup account
If your Mac is at home, the most popular connection option is to get an account with an Internet service

provider (ISP), a firm like MacUnlimited, Demon
Internet or BT Internet that enables you to connect
to the Net through its computer servers. (Many ISPs
require you to pay a monthly subscription; others,
such as MacUnlimited, are subscription-free and get
a share of the telephone call charge you're normally
paying anyway. Which method, and indeed which
ISP, is best for you depends on many factors, such
as how long you'll spend online each month and
whether you need Mac-specialist technical support.
Such questions, however, are outside the scope of
this book.) These accounts connect your Mac to the
Net through your modem (built-in in all modern
Macs) over a telephone line.

Most ISPs provide a CD-ROM that automatically
installs the software you need, then enters the
necessary settings into the correct places for you,
including the phone number your Mac needs to dial
to connect to the Net. Some ISP CD-ROMs do not
support Macintosh at all, however, which means
you may need to download your own software and
configure it manually. Some others have software
designed for older versions of the Mac OS. This
means you need to start your Mac in Mac OS 9
(which you should also have on your hard disk

Mac OS X makes it as
easy as possible to set
up an Internet
connection on your Mac,
enabling you to enjoy
Websites, e-mail and
many other online
services.

See also

Full details of the
settings you need to
note down in Mac OS 9
are in the chapter
"Before You Start" on
page 33. If you have an
existing dialup account
that you're happy with,
it can be less trouble to
copy settings over and
set up your OS X
connection manually.

if you've followed our installation procedure), and
use the CD-ROM here. Once the account is working
correctly, you can note down the settings in Mac OS
9, then re-enter into them in the appropriate spots in
Mac OS X.

Alternatively, contact the ISP and ask them if it is
possible to open an account with them via their
Web page. If you can get access to the Web through
work or a friend, you can then choose your e-mail
address, enter your credit card details for payment
(if the ISP requires this) and get the settings you
need via the Web service. Even then, however, the
option may not work entirely: while Freeserve, for
example, offers an online facility to open an
account, the procedure includes an automatic check
that you have a BT phone line – and this check
works only with PCs running Windows. If all goes
according to plan, though, you can create your
account via the Web, and note down the settings
as you go, ready to enter into Mac OS X later.

Unless your Internet
service provider offers
a connection CD that
works directly in Mac
OS X, you will need to
enter your Internet
settings yourself.

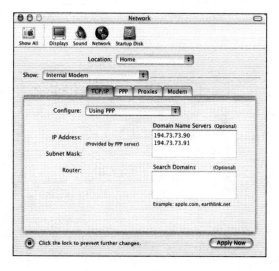

Broadband accounts

Broadband is a higher-speed connection made over
a telephone line or cable, but so far it's available
only in a few urban centres in the UK, and it might
never be available everywhere. (This is because it
requires special equipment at the exchange as well
as at your end, and can be affected by your distance
from the exchange and the quality of the line,
among other factors.) It is also more expensive than
a normal dialup account. Those providers which
offer broadband typically prefer at present to visit
your home or office to install the equipment and
software you need. Some do not currently support
Macs, or do so only half-heartedly.

Most domestic broadband connections currently
rely on an external modem that links to your Mac's
USB modem. Whether this will work with Mac OS
X depends on whether the modem manufacturer
has provided a USB driver: the operating system
won't recognise the modem's presence without it.
Check with your ISP for availability, as well as the
manufacturer's Website. You may be lucky enough
to have a broadband connection linked through
your Mac's Ethernet port, in which case no driver is
required. Ethernet-based links are usually available
through broadband accounts for business users.

Quick tip

Is your broadband
connection over USB?
At the time of writing, all
UK ADSL providers
install the same model of
broadband modem (as
supplied by BT), the
Alcatel SpeedTouch
USB. Alcatel, the world's
leading supplier of USB
broadband modems, has
promised to release a
Mac OS X driver for this
model, and it is expected
by the time you read
this. Visit the Website
www.alcateldsl.com
for the latest details.

There's always one, isn't
there? The Internet
service provider AOL
follows its own set of
rules for connecting your
Mac to the Net, but it's
easy to get started.

AOL

There is a major exception to the procedure for setting up ISP accounts, and that's the well-known service provider AOL. This firm not only provides access to the Web, but also offers its own online content, exclusively for AOL customers. AOL also uses its own software for creating an account and later connecting, which bypasses the standard settings and systems in Mac OS X or, indeed, any other operating system.

Like some other ISPs, AOL offers initial setup software on CD-ROM which you will need to use in Mac OS 9. Once you have a working AOL connection, you can then download a version of the AOL application for Mac OS X. (For more details if you're already with AOL, launch the AOL software and enter the keyword "Mac".) When you install this download in Mac OS X and run the software, it will automatically copy all the settings you need to connect from the equivalent software package you installed under Mac OS 9. At no point should you need to enter any further settings yourself.

AOL is popular for its exclusive content and for its software's "parental controls", which can help parents regulate what kids are able to see and

To see QuickTime movies within Web pages, choose your correct connection speed from the QuickTime area in System Preferences.

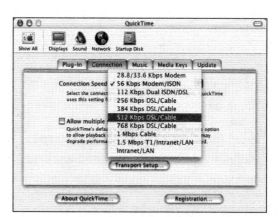

do on the Net. However, the Web browser part of
the AOL software, which enables you to visit the
rest of the Web outside AOL itself, has in the past
lagged behind and created compatibility problems
with some sites. What's worse, because AOL's
software bypasses the standard systems for
connecting to the Net, it has caused problems for
people who want to use other accounts and other
software after installing AOL. It's too soon to say
whether there will be any such problems under
OS X, however, and AOL might be fine for you.

Connecting through a network

In most offices, Macs and other computers are
linked together so they're able to exchange
information, and then all link through the same
high-speed Internet connection. Most of these local
networks rely on Ethernet, although a growing
number use wireless connections as well. In most
cases, your firm will have a technical support team
or manager to set up and maintain your Mac and
its Internet connection; this is likely to be the
department that made the decision to switch
you to Mac OS X in the first place.

Remote Access

Your company may also permit you to connect to its
servers from outside the office, connecting through
a modem to a phone number provided by your
company. Remote Access enables you to check your
work e-mail and sometimes to access the Web and
other areas of the Internet.

All of the above

It's also possible to share an Internet connection
across several Macs in a smaller network, including
home networks. For example, your main Mac may
have a direct Internet link to which your second
Mac can also link via Ethernet or AirPort. To enable
you to do this, some IP addresses have been set
aside for exclusive use in local networks, enabling
you to tell one computer from another on your

network without interfering with any Internet connections you might have set up. The ranges of IP addresses you're allowed to use are 10.x.x.x and 192.168.x.x, where x is any number between 0 and 999. So, for example, you might give one Mac the IP address 10.0.0.1, the next 10.0.0.2 and so on; only the Mac with the Internet connection has a "legitimate" IP address.

A place to start

In the section "Welcome to Mac OS X", we saw how you can transfer existing settings from your older version of the Mac OS and enter them in Mac OS X's Setup Assistant. Mac OS X also provides a place to alter those settings later or add new ones: the Network area in System Preferences. The starting point for your Internet configuration is to choose your Location, which in broad terms establishes where your Mac is and therefore which collection of settings it should use.

Locations are primarily designed for users of portable computers: if you take your PowerBook or iBook to several different places of work (or from work to home) and want to access the Internet from each, you may have different settings for each place – a dialup connection at home, for instance, and a connection via the Ethernet network in the office.

You can keep Mac OS X up to date with regular checks over the Internet for any additions that Apple has released, and download them to update your system.

Just create a new Location for each place, and you can switch between them as you move about. Locations are also useful if you use more than one Internet service provider at home, a practice many heavy users of the Net follow nowadays. Creating a Location for each ISP means you can store several groups of settings and switch between them at will.

The first thing you need to do, then, is to create a Location, which might be "Home" or "Work" or use an ISP's name like "MacUnlimited". The Location name at the top of the Network area is a pull-down menu, which includes the option to create a new location. If your Mac remains in one place and you use just one ISP, you can stick with the Location called "Automatic" that's already provided.

The choice of Automatic as the default location name hints at another feature of Mac OS X's Internet settings, which is the ability to detect how you are connecting to the Net and choose the appropriate setting from those you've entered. If you have a modem plugged in, the Mac will try to use that; if you have an Ethernet cable plugged in instead, the Mac will switch settings. This is great

Mac upgraders

The Network area in System Preferences consolidates several Mac OS 9 Control Panels – Location Manager, Modem, Remote Access and TCP/IP – into a single, integrated arrangement.

Quick tip

The fastest way to change Location is to go to **Location** in your Apple menu, where you'll find a list of the Locations you've created to choose from.

Microsoft Internet Explorer is Mac OS X's default Web browser, enabling you to visit the Apple Website and the millions more out there. (You are of course free to install and use your own preferred browser software instead.)

Quick tip

If you wish, you can set the order in which Mac OS X checks your configurations for a working connection. In System Preferences, click on Network. If applicable, use Location to choose the location you want to set the priorities on. Then in the Show pull-down, select the option Show Active Network Ports. This shows a sub-window listing every port you have set up – typically modem, Ethernet, and possibly AirPort. As a note in the window explains, you can simply drag port options up or down the list to change the order in which Mac OS X checks them.

if you have a laptop you use with a modem at home and through a network in the office, in which case you have two Internet accounts.

Below the Location pull-down menu is the Configure pull-down menu, which gives you access to the settings for individual networking ports, such as your modem or your Ethernet port. Your AirPort card will also appear here if you are using one.

Configuring Internal Modem

This is where you can set up a connection to your ISP, or Remote Access to your office network if you have it. There are four tabs for you to enter information into; this is where you'll need your notes of your Internet settings in Mac OS 9 or from your online ISP registration.

TCP/IP

With a standard dialup account, you're usually given a different IP address automatically each time you connect, so if you choose the option Configure Using PPP, you won't be given the option to enter an IP address. If you have company remote access,

Choose one of these TV channels in QuickTime Player to see live broadcasts and video highlights over the Net. (The quality will depend on the speed of your Net connection, though.)

you have an IP address to enter, so choose the option Configure Manually and enter the IP sequence. You may have at least one Domain Name Server address, or DNS as Mac OS 9 refers to them, to enter. You may also have a Search Domain to enter, but don't worry if you haven't been provided with one: they're not essential to get you connected.

PPP

You'll need to enter details into the PPP tab if you're using an ISP or Remote Access. If you've copied settings from Mac OS 9, these are the details that you took from the Remote Access Control Panel. Use the Service Provider field simply for labelling. The Telephone Number field should include any area codes; don't use any brackets or dashes. Your ISP may have given you a second number to enter in case the first is engaged; enter this in Alternate Number. You should also enter your account user name and its corresponding password. If you don't want to have to verify your password each time you connect to the Internet, tick Save Password.

The PPP Options button in this area reveals a further set of choices to make, although it's not vital that you tinker with these. You may want to open an Internet connection automatically on starting a

Apple's free iTools service enables you to send electronic postcards, create your own Web home page and receive e-mail through your own Mac.com address.

Web browser or e-mail program, or to disconnect after a set period of inactivity, which could save on your phone bill.

Proxies

This tab enables you to set up alternative servers for your Mac to use when it uses certain Internet protocols, which can sometimes speed up access. If you haven't been provided with any proxies by your ISP, don't worry.

Modem

Just glance at the Modem tab to make sure you're happy with the choices. The vast majority of Macs using Mac OS X connect through the Mac's built-in modem, listed here under the name "Apple Internal Modem". Use the pull-down menu to select your model if this isn't the case. Decide whether you want the modem to make its tell-tale bleeps and screeches as confirmation that it's working, and make sure that the Dialing option is set to Tone, which is designed for the touch-tone phone system that most phone lines are now based on.

Keep tabs on your modem-based Internet link with Internet Connect: it shows you how long you've been online and how busy your connection is.

Configuring a broadband modem

If you connect to the Internet through a broadband
modem, you must create a new configuration to
store the settings you require. From the Show pull-
down menu in Network, select Active Network
Ports, then duplicate the Internal Modem port,
which provides the template for your broadband
modem connection. You can name the configuration
something like "Broadband Modem" to make its
use plain. This configuration uses the same tabs as
the Internal Modem setup covered above, but some
of the settings you should make are subtly different.
Make sure you install your modem driver before
you configure the connection.

TCP/IP

As in the case of a modem connection, you are
unlikely to have an IP address to enter, so choose
Configure Using PPP from the pull-down menu.
You may have at least one Domain Name Server
sequence and a search domain to enter.

PPP

Your ISP should have provided a user name and
password for you to enter here, and should also
instruct you what to enter under Number. This may
be a single-digit number, typically 0, or a server
name. Broadband links don't actually use a phone
number, so don't be alarmed at the discrepancy.

Proxies

If you haven't been provided with any proxies by
your ISP, ignore this tab.

Modem

Use the modem pull-down in this area to select the
modem model plugged into your USB port, which
will be included in the list of choices if you installed
the driver software earlier. You should also untick
the checkbox "Wait for dial tone before dialling".

Configuring Built-In Ethernet

You may connect to the Net through your Ethernet
port rather than, or as well as, your modem. As
we've seen, Mac OS X can detect which port you're
using, and you can use the Advanced option to set
the order in the OS checks the ports. So if you have
a modem connection at home and a network
connection in the office, you can simply now enter
your office settings into the Configuration named
"Built-In Ethernet". Again, there are four tabs to
work through:

TCP/IP

This is the network equivalent of the TCP/IP tab
you may already have set up under Internal Modem
(see above). As in that tab, you have fields for IP
addresses, Domain Name Servers and optional
Search Domains. If you use an office network, it's
likely that you will been allocated a specific IP
address, which you should enter here.

PPPoE

PPPoE is the broadband equivalent of the PPP
technology you use to connect through a modem;
the oE component stands simply for "over Ethernet". You should configure this area if your
broadband connection is through your Ethernet
port, as is the case with most business accounts.
The essentials you need here are your account user
name and password; your ISP will advise you if
any other settings are necessary.

AppleTalk

You need to make the AppleTalk networking system
active before your connection will work. Larger
networks are split into smaller zones to make
maintenance easier, and your tech support team or
manager can indicate which network zone you
belong to. All the options available to you are given
in the AppleTalk Zone pull-down menu.

Proxies

These are alternative servers for your Mac to use
when it uses certain Internet protocols, which can
sometimes speed up access. If you haven't been
provided with any proxies, you can safely ignore
this tab.

Advanced settings

With these settings entered, your Internet
connection should be ready to work. There are two
other areas within System Preferences where you
can enhance the way your connection works:

Internet

This area's main role is when you decide you want
to share some key preferences across several
different Internet programs. Many people, however,
still prefer to set up each application individually.
Still, there are a few items here worth anyone's
attention, scattered across four tabs.

If you entered the details of your existing iTools
account or signed up for a new one during your
initial installation of Mac OS X, you'll find your
details neatly entered under the iTools tab. If you
passed up the chance earlier, this pane is your
opportunity to register your account. Click the Free
Sign-up button to open a Web browser and view a
Web page for registration; make sure first that your
Internet settings are entered.

The most important option in the Email tab is at
the top. Some applications, notably Web browsers,
provide an option to send an e-mail, perhaps by
clicking on a link. When you do this, an e-mail
program on your Mac's hard disk is opened and a
new message addressed to the appropriate recipient
appears. If you have more than one e-mail program
on your Mac, choose your favourite in the Default
pull-down menu.

Similarly, many programs can automatically activate a Web browser and open a nominated Web page. Use the Web tab to choose which browser of those installed should be opened.

With many Websites offering forum boards for discussion, fewer people are using newsgroups, an Internet facility that has traditionally provided thousands of meeting points to satisfy different interests. If you still use a newsgroup browser, however, choose it from the pull-down menu here. You can also enter the news server address supplied by your ISP or support team.

QuickTime

Many Websites offer video clips for you to watch: sometimes they're finite clips embedded into Web pages, which you normally have to download to your hard disk to watch; sometimes they're ongoing or "streaming" broadcasts, like watching TV on your Mac. With either of these techniques, the Website may offer the same footage at several different levels of quality, to cater for the wide variance in access speeds that different people enjoy. The idea is that people with slow connections aren't frustrated by waiting perhaps hours to see a clip (or suffering a lot of dropped frames in a streaming clip), while those with faster connections get the best-possible quality. The Connection tab under QuickTime is where you can set the quality level that best suits your connection.

Of the choices presented in the Connection Speed pull-down menu, the least you should choose is 56Kbps Modem/ISDN: every Mac recommended for use with Mac OS X has this speed of modem built-in. If you have an ISDN connection, choose 56Kbps Modem/ISDN if you have a single-channel or 64Kbps connection, or 112Kbps ISDN/DSL if you have a dual-channel or 128Kbps link. Check with your ISP if you're not sure which you have. The various DSL/Cable options are for broadband connections. The vast majority of broadband links in use today have a maximum "downstream" speed of 512Kbps, so that is your most likely choice. Check with your ISP if you're not sure what your connection speed is, though. If your Internet access is through an office network, choose the bottom option of Intranet/LAN.

The Allow Multiple Simultaneous Streams checkbox will let you play more than one streaming or ongoing broadcast at once. This may cause stuttering reception on slower connections. When you choose your connection speed, the tick box below will tick or untick itself in response, and you'll get the best result if you don't overrule this automatic decision. The Connection pane also includes the Transport Setup button, which leads to advanced options that are no concern to most people. You may need to reconfigure the port ID described here if you are receiving video through a private network, but the settings here are fine for everyday Web access.

Firewalls

One of Mac OS X's most powerful Internet features is actually hidden from view – unless you know how to look for it. A firewall is a system that attempts to prevent people from gaining access to your Mac and the information on it via the Internet without your knowledge or permission. As the Net has grown, so too has the notoriety of hackers, people who try to break into supposedly secure computer setups. The most common targets for such attempts are the powerful computer servers powering the biggest Websites, but it is technically possible for any personal computer connected to the Internet to be attacked. Don't get this out of proportion, though: most people will use a computer their whole lives without facing such an attack. Still, a firewall can be a robust first line

Quick tip

If you use AOL for your Internet access, it won't work through a firewall, so you will have to switch off the firewall each time you use AOL.

of defence against the tide of hacker attacks –
and with the right tools, it's easy to set one up
in Mac OS X.

A firewall insulates your Mac against a hacker's
ability to exploit the way different systems on the
Internet work alongside each other. There are many
different ways to send and receive information over
the Net: it might be a Web page, an e-mail, a file
download or a live chat channel. Each different
access protocol has been allocated its own number,
known as a port ID. Any information sent as a Web
page, for example, travels across the port ID 80,
while FTP (File Transfer Protocol), used for many
file downloads, is allocated port ID 21. For every
port ID with such a major role, though, there are
thousands more that are rarely needed. By using
software that burrows through one of the rarely-
used port IDs, the hacker is able to gain access to
your Mac. A firewall blocks all the port IDs that you
don't use, massively reducing the opportunities
available to a hacker.

Mac OS X includes a firewall in its basic System
software, but it's set up with every port ID open.
While it's possible to use the Terminal application
to onfigure the firewall yourself, it's a task best left
to experts. Besides, you can buy an application that
will help you set up a firewall in minutes, with no
expert knowledge required. Two such applications
are BrickHouse and Firewall X, available to
download via **www.versiontracker.com**. Each
program gives you a list of port IDs and asks you
which ones you want to use, then closes the rest.
The advantage of these programs is that you don't
have to know which port ID is used by which
technology: you just tell the program you want to
use the Web, FTP and e-mail, for example, and it
does the rest. Once your firewall is set up, it's
permanent until you decide to deactivate or alter it,
which you can do through the same application.

Things to do, places to see

Many areas of Mac OS X can now take advantage
of your Internet connection once it's set up; here's
a summary of what you can do:

Browse the Web
Microsoft's Internet Explorer program enables you
to view any Web page, then add any you like to a
list of Favorites which you can use as shortcuts to
those pages later. You can also download files such
as applications that you find on the Web. (There
are of course other browsers you can opt to use
instead if you prefer, and other means of downloading files as well.)

Check your e-mail
Mail is designed to help you send e-mail messages
and check for them, and can work across several
e-mail accounts. (Again, there are alternative e-mail
applications which you are free to choose.)

Discover new software
Mac OS X already includes a great selection of
programs, but there are thousands more available,
with more announced daily. To see the latest
applications on offer, activate your Internet
connection, then select **Get Mac OS Software**
in your Apple menu.

Get a clue
The Help Viewer is Mac OS X's built-in tool for
providing answers to any questions you might
have about the operating system or applications.
Many of its answers are stored on the Internet, so
that they can be updated with current information.
If you search for an answer for a problem and find
that the option you click on won't display, you may
need to make your Internet connection active to
view the answer.

Quick tip

In Mail, select **Mail >
Preferences** to create
and configure your
e-mail account, using
the settings supplied by
your ISP or company
tech support team.

Keep Mac OS X up to date

Apple periodically offers small-scale updates to improve performance or fix bugs; Mac OS X is able to detect these through the Internet, then download and install them automatically. There are two areas in System Preferences within which you can control the automated update procedure:

Software Update monitors the availability of improvements to the operating system itself. You can choose whether to check for updates automatically or to make a manual check when you remember. If you decide on automatic checks, you can pick a time of day and decide how frequently the check should be made. (Weekly is more than adequate: the updates aren't that frequent.) Your Internet connection must be open at that time for the check to work.

QuickTime Update offers similar manual or automatic checks for updated software used by the QuickTime media player system. You can look out for both QuickTime updates and enhancements offered by other firms, such as video compression files that offer higher-quality video clips. If you choose the automatic update option, the QuickTime Player application will check for updates whenever it is running and you have an active Internet connection. Click on the Updates tab in the QuickTime pane to make your choice.

Play live movies and music

There are dozens of TV stations and hundreds of radio stations now broadcasting material over the Net. You can use a Web browser like Internet Explorer to seek them out, of course, but Mac OS X offers two applications with direct links to some of the most popular material available:

QuickTime Player enables you to watch more than a dozen Internet-based TV stations, including household names like the BBC, CNN and MTV.

Some stations offer live 24-hour coverage, while others provide regularly updated short clips. Open QuickTime Player and make sure your Internet connection is active, then click on the TV button in the player window to see the selection of stations available for you to choose from.

iTunes gives you access to dozens of live radio channels, all broadcast over the Net. Open iTunes and make sure your Internet connection is active, then click on the Radio Tuner option in the Source window to see a list of available channels. Just choose the station you want to start listening!

Publish on the Web
Mac OS X ostensibly offers two ways to publish your own material on the Web as well as just visiting other sites – but in practice, one method is not a good idea. It's possible to present your own Web material to others through Mac OS X and its Web Sharing feature. The only reason we're mentioning it here, though, is to advise against using the facility to deliver material to a wide audience over the Internet: your connection isn't designed for this task. If you want to publish something on the Web, stick to the existing practices of leasing space from a hosting firm for large projects, or using the free Webspace offered by most ISPs for more personal-scale pages.

And in fact, Mac OS X gives you direct access to even more Webspace where you can easily publish a simple home page, as an alternative or a complement to your ISP's Webspace. Home Page is one of the features of iTools, Apple's free suite of online services. If you have an iTools account, you can use tools at the iTools site to create a page with text, photos and even video, hosted on Apple's own Web servers. Visit **www.apple.com/itools** for all the details.

See also

Web Sharing is designed to help you share material across intranets or private computer networks, such as the one in your office. You can find more details in the Guided Tour "Sharing Your Mac" on page 155.

Store files on the Net
If you have an iTools account, you can store files
on your iDisk, your personal storage volume on
Apple's servers accessible over the Internet. Enter
your iTools settings in the Internet area of System
Preferences, then activate your Internet connection.
You can open your iDisk using the icon in the
Finder toolbar or by selecting **Go > iDisk**.

Tell the right time
You can synchronise your Mac's clock against a
super-accurate chronometer over the Internet.
Choose Date & Time in System Preferences, then
click the Network Time tab for controls that enable
you to choose a network time server and check
the time.

Helping hand

Further options in Mac OS X enable you to
maintain your Internet connection and keep
track of associated information:

Monitoring your connection
Internet Connect enables you to open or close
your modem connection and presents helpful
information like the length of time you've been on
and the activity taking place on your connection.
You can also keep tabs using the PPP or PPPoE
Menu Extras.

Storing your e-mail contacts
Address Book integrates with Mail to store any
e-mail address belonging to a contact. Use the
Address Book option in Mail's toolbar to look
up the address you need.

Storing your Internet passwords
Many Websites and other Internet services require
you to maintain a private user name and password,
without which you cannot access the service.

Use Keychain Access to store all your settings, then
protect the entire list with a password only you
know. Easier than trying to remember a dozen
separate passwords and usernames.

Instant Web access
If there's a Website you can't last five minutes
without visiting, you can keep a link to it in your
Dock. In Internet Explorer, Websites stored in the
Organize Favorites window or the Favorites toolbar
have an icon resembling an @ sign next to them;
there's also one in the address bar when you are
visiting a site. Drag the icon next to the site you
want on to the right side of the Dock to create a
direct link to that site. (This doesn't create a copy
of the site on your hard disk or download its
content to you; it's just a link you can click on
to access the site easily.)

22 Go Go Gadget

As capable as your Mac is in its own right, its
powers are enhanced enormously by the addition
of external devices. Many of us love our gadgets,
whether it's a digital camera, a portable MP3 player
for listening to music, or a printer for putting files
onto paper. Your Mac plays a vital role at the centre
of your collection of devices, taking information
from some to manipulate as only a Mac can, then
sending the improved result through another device
for your use.

Device drivers

Mac OS X is able to detect external devices as
you plug them in, making them ready to use
immediately. To do this, it refers to a small file
known as a driver, which contains details of what
the device does and how it works with electronic
information. No external device can be recognised
without a driver. Mac OS X includes hundreds of
drivers that enable it to recognise many common
devices, without any effort on your part: just plug
the device into the relevant connection port, such as
your Mac's USB or FireWire ports, and it's ready to
work. You can also install further drivers, perhaps
to support the special features of particular devices,

if your device manufacturer has written them; these may be included on a CD with the device when you buy it, or you may find drivers at the maker's Website or through the Version Tracker Website at **www.versiontracker.com**.

As we'll see shortly, some devices do require an additional setup procedure, and Mac OS X also offers several applications designed to help you get more from your gadgets.

Your storage media

You've got to have somewhere to keep all those applications, documents and other files, and your hard disk isn't always enough by itself. Mac OS X is able to recognise a variety of external storage devices, including Zip drives, SuperDisk drives, CD writers and additional hard disk drives. Your Mac may also have some of these devices built-in.

Preparing your storage

Any storage medium must use a disk format that Mac OS X can recognise before it can write files onto it. Most media you buy nowadays are already formatted in DOS format, which is used by PCs running Microsoft Windows, but the best format for your Mac is called Mac OS Extended format. To reformat a storage medium, open Disk Utility in **Applications/Utilities** and select the appropriate

Mac upgraders

If you have a device driver created for use under Mac OS 9, it won't work under Mac OS X. One of the operating system's built-in drivers may recognise the device, but you may need to get a new driver from the manufacturer. Visit your manufacturer's Website to see if OS X drivers are available.

Mac OS X makes it easy to connect your Mac to a wide variety of other electronic devices, including Apple's iPod digital music player. Photo courtesy of Apple.

Quick tip

If you'll need to later use a disk in a Mac running Mac OS 9, tick the checkbox "Install Mac OS 9 Drivers" when re-formatting it. To later use a disk in a Mac running a version of the Mac OS older than 8.6, choose Mac OS Standard from the Volume Format pull-down menu. This menu also includes disk formats suitable for PCs running Microsoft Windows or Unix.

Quick tip

If you have a CD-RW you want to erase and use again, you can erase it like any other storage volume using Disk Utility.

Mac OS X's ColorSync uses device profiles to ensure that the colours on a picture you scan into your Mac look the same on-screen and when you print it out.

disk from the list on the left of the window. Click on the Erase tab and choose Mac OS Extended from the Volume Format pull-down menu. You can also name the disk if you want. Beware, though: reformatting any storage medium means erasing it, so you lose any data already stored on it.

Writing CDs

One exception to this standard procedure is when you use writable CDs, such as CD-Rs and CD-RWs. These discs are not formatted when you buy them, so Mac OS X will prepare the disc for use when you first insert it in your CD writer drive. An icon representing the CD appears on the Desktop, enabling you to copy files onto it like any other storage volume. The information is not physically transferred onto the CD until you're ready to eject it. When you drag the CD onto the Trash icon or select **File > Eject**, you're asked if you now wish to write the files onto the CD (or "burn" the CD). You can eject without writing the disc if you choose. You can also write the CD at any time by clicking the Burn option in the Finder window toolbar.

Disk images

You can convert any storage volume into a disk image, which resides on a another volume but

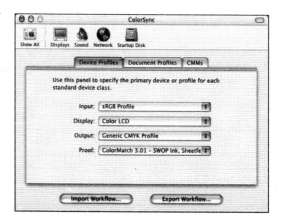

imitates the behaviour of the original, enabling you to view and activate files held on the disk image. If you have a CD that you make frequent copies of, for example, you can convert it to a disk image and use this as the template for further copies, so you don't have to keep the original CD to hand. You can also create blank disk images and add files to them yourself just as if they were real volumes.

To make a disk image, open the Disk Copy application stored in **Applications/Utilities.** In the Image menu, you can choose to create a blank disk image or create one based on an available storage volume. If you're making a blank image, you must choose its storage capacity. You change the capacity later by selecting **Image > Convert Image**. You can also choose where to save the disk image; the volume you choose must have enough free space to store the entire capacity of the disk image, even if you're not using all of it at present.

To activate a disk image, double-click on its container file: Disk Copy will "mount" the disk image so it is available like any other storage volume. You can see it on your Desktop and alongside your other volumes in the Computer area in your Finder window. You can treat this volume like any other, double-clicking on it to view its contents and adding or removing files and folders. When you have finished working with your disk image volume, highlight the volume icon and select **File > Eject**. This removes the icon and saves the current state of the disk image for later access.

Your printer

Practically every Mac user wants to publish a document on paper from time to time, while many need paper printouts many times a day. That's why a printer is an essential component of your Mac setup, and Mac OS X is able to work with hundreds

Quick tip

You can encrypt any disk image as you create it, so that you have to enter a password to access the image later. This prevents anyone else from viewing the disk image's contents. Choose your preferred protection method from the Encryption pull-down menu as you create the disk image file.

Quick tip

Disk Copy enables you to press a disk image onto a writable CD that behaves like the disk image itself. Select **Image > Burn Image**.

See also

For more on setting
networks and choosing
connection protocols,
see the Guided Tour
"Sharing Your Mac"
on page 155.

Quick tip

If you place Print Center
in your Dock, you can
see the status of your
selected printer, for
example if it's printing
out a document or has
a document queued up
for printing.

of different models. As with other devices, Mac OS
X is able to detect a printer as soon as you connect
one to your Mac, whether it's linked through USB
or Ethernet. Drivers for many printer models from
Canon, Epson and Hewlett-Packard are installed
as part of Mac OS X, including these firms' most
popular inkjet and laser models.

The Print Center application, stored in **Applications
/Utilities**, is able to detect a printer as you plug it
in. You may still need to open the application to
select the printer for use, especially if you are
connected to a network with access to several
printers. In Print Center, you can see a window
listing all nominated printers available to you.
Click the Add Printer button to select a further
model. The Printer List window that opens offers
three connection methods in a pull-down menu.
The options LPR Using IP and AppleTalk cater for
printers connected through your Ethernet port;
choose the former option if your network is based
on TCP/IP and the latter option if your network
employs AppleTalk.

The third pull-down menu option is USB, which
obviously shows printers connected through your
USB port. Whichever connection method you use,
the Printer List window presents every printer it
can detect, although models that lack a compatible
printer driver on your Mac are listed as
unsupported and are not available to select.

When you connect your
digital camera to your
Mac, Image Capture
opens to give you
immediate access to the
pictures you've taken.

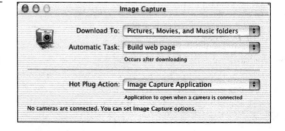

Click on the name of the printer you want; you can use the Printer Model pull-down menu to choose a printer driver if you are not happy with the automatic choice that Mac OS X makes. Click the Add button to place the printer on your main list in the Print Center window, then click on the printer in that list to make it available.

Printing a document

Most applications offer an option to print out the document you are working in right now, typically in the File menu. Before you print your first document, though, you should select the nearby Page Setup option: this enables you to confirm the size of the paper sheets you have inserted into your printer. This enables your application to accurately show you how the the document will appear before you print it out. The options available in your Page Setup window can vary by application, but you are typically able to set paper sizes for each printer available to your Mac, or for individual paper trays in a printer if there are more than one. You can also choose to scale down the document, which makes it print out at a smaller size.

When your document is ready, you can select the Print option. Again, the available options vary by

Hook up your FireWire digital video camera to your Mac and use iMovie to turn your raw footage into a professional-looking movie.

application, but you should expect to be able to choose which printer you are using, how many copies to print out, and which pages in a multi-page document you can print. More detailed options may include the ability to change your printout layout, enabling you to fit more than one document page on a sheet of paper, conserving paper while you are making preliminary checks on your work.

You should also see a Preview button, which opens the document you are working on in the Preview application, so that you can see exactly how the document will appear when you print it out. While in Preview, you can opt to save the document as a PDF file, which you can open later in Preview or pass to other computer users for them to open in Adobe Acrobat Reader.

ColorSync

Devices such as scanners, digital cameras and printers can combine with your Mac to create a production line of technology dedicated to creating material for publication, for example in print on the Web. If you're a professional designer – or just picky – it's important that you get the results you expect: if you use photos in a design project, you want the finished picture to look like the original, not some washed-out imitation. If you're designing a logo, you want it to show the same colour on a computer screen as in a printed brochure.

Mac OS X's ColorSync technology helps keep colours consistent across a variety of devices as you create your material. You can set a ColorSync profile for each device used in your workflow; Mac OS X interprets these profiles so that the shade of red you scan from a photo using your scanner looks correct on your display, and prints out in the same red on your colour printer. When you buy a printer, digital camera or scanner, you should have a ColorSync

profile for that device included with its software
package; you may also find ColorSync profiles at
the manufacturer's Website.

Mac OS X is able to detect ColorSync profiles stored
in any of these locations:

Library/ColorSync/Profiles
Any user can access profiles stored here, but only
users with Administrator privileges can add or
remove profiles.

~/Library/ColorSync/Profiles
Only you can access profiles stored in this location
within your Home folder.

System/Library/ColorSync/Profiles
No user is allowed to add or remove profiles
in this location.

To use ColorSync to its fullest extent, you need to
choose profiles for each relevant device connected
to your Mac. You typically have an input source,
such as a scanner or digital camera; an output
source, such as a printer; and the display you use
while working on your Mac. To set profiles for each
of these sources, open System Preferences and click
ColorSync. The Device Profiles tab presents pull-
down menus for choosing profiles for each source;
there's a fourth menu for a proofer, an advanced
device used in professional design for printing the
finished document at a quality comparable to that
of commercial printing.

Two further tabs give you more precise control.
Some documents used in design applications can
store their own profiles to describe how your Mac
should treat colour separations. A printer, for
example, has only four ink colours, so a separation
profile describes how those four colours should be
used to create the full range of colours on a page.
The Embedded Profiles tab enables you to choose

Mac upgraders

If you installed a
ColorSync profile for a
device in Mac OS 9, you
can use the same profile
in Mac OS X; copy the
profile to one of the
ColorSync folders used
by Mac OS X.

Quick tip

If you are on a network,
you can store or access
ColorSync profiles stored
at **Network/Library/
ColorSync/Profiles**.

Quick tip

If you work in a group,
you can share a set of
ColorSync profiles,
known as a workflow,
among everyone in the
group. In the ColorSync
area of System
Preferences, click the
Export Workflow button
to create a file that you
can distribute to your
colleagues. To load a
workflow document
you've received, click the
Import Workflow button.

which profiles your Mac should use if the document
does not include its own, and offers pull-down
menus for the four main types of colour separation.
The CMMs tab enables you to choose a colour
matching system to control the whole process.

You may also need to set your application to use
ColorSync; check your application's preferences.

Mac OS X includes three applications to assist your
use of ColorSync, all stored in **Applications/
Utilities**. ColorSync Utility can check a profile for
errors and make any necessary repairs; Display
Calibrator helps you create a profile for your Mac's
individual display; and DigitalColor Meter helps
you check that the colours on your display are
being presented accurately.

Your digital camera

Mac OS X is able to automatically interact with
many digital cameras plugged in your Mac's USB
port, including recent models from Canon, Fuji,
Kodak, Olympus and Sony. The Image Capture
application detects your camera as you plug it in
and presents small thumbnail images of all the
photos now stored on the camera. You can do some
simple housekeeping like deleting unwanted
images or rotating pictures, then copy any photos
you want over to your Mac. All images go straight
into your Pictures folder.

Your digital video camera

Mac OS X can interact with many digital video
camcorders plugged into your Mac's FireWire port.
The iMovie application is able to show footage
transferred through the camera, whether you're
filming live or playing back material you recorded
earlier. With iMovie, you can edit this raw footage

into a presentable form, adding transition effects between clips, then add soundtrack music and titles. iMovie can save the final result as a Quick-Time movie on your Mac or transfer the video back onto your camera (assuming that the camera is capable of receiving an incoming signal – some camcorders sold in Europe have this feature disabled because it would put them in a higher tax category and thus make them more expensive).

Your MP3 player and music CDs

Mac OS X places your Mac at the heart of your music collection, enabling you to combine your favourite songs from your CDs with fresh sounds downloaded from the Internet, then transfer compilations onto different media. Most of this activity centres around the application iTunes. You can insert a music CD into your Mac's CD drive and play it using iTunes, then transfer your favourite songs to iTunes' music library, which stores tracks in the digital MP3 format on your hard disk. If you download free MP3s from Websites, you can also place these in your library.

As you create playlists in iTunes of your favourite compilations, you can transfer music onto other media so you can listen to them away from your Mac. You can copy the songs onto a CD-R using your CD writer: insert the disc, choose your list of songs in iTunes and hit the application's Burn button. You can play the result in any standard audio CD player. iTunes can also detect the most popular MP3 player models, such as Diamond's recent Rio players and Creative Labs' Jukebox, enabling you to transfer songs from your library onto your portable player. Just plug the MP3 player into your USB port, and it should appear in iTunes' window. And, naturally, iTunes integrates perfectly with Apple's own MP3 player, the breathtaking iPod. See Apple's Website for more information.

Quick tip

If your camera is capable of storing video or sound clips, Image Capture can transfer these to your Mac. The application can also recognise some card readers, which accept the data storage cards on which many cameras hold images. These are often more convenient to use than plugging in the cameras.

Quick tip

Apple's iPod can also be used as an external hard disk to store or transport your files: click on the iPod tab at the bottom right of the iTunes 2 screen and you'll get the option to make it visible as a storage volume. Then you simply drag files into it like any other removable volume.

23 Living with the Legacy

Mac OS X is at once a brand-new operating system and the inheritor of a proud legacy: millions of people have enjoyed the Mac and its operating system since 1984. In this chapter, we look at bringing that inheritance into Mac OS X.

Welcome to Classic

Mac OS X shouldn't be able to directly open and run applications written for older versions of the Mac OS, such are the underlying differences between old and new. There is a tool built into Mac OS X, though, that sidesteps this fundamental incompatibility so that you can in fact run older programs in Mac OS X. Its name is Classic, and its purpose is to behave as much like an older Mac OS version as possible.

When you attempt to use an older Mac application, typically by double-clicking on it, Mac OS X is able to respond to this by switching to Classic. The tool works by starting up the older Mac OS 9, which you must have on your hard disk alongside Mac OS X. You'll see a window appear in Mac OS X that represents Mac OS 9 starting up, complete with

the messages familiar to anyone who used a Mac
before Mac OS X was released.

Once this second operating system has started up,
it remains active but invisible, until you open any
application designed to work under the older Mac
OS. At this point, you'll see the program load just
as it would if your Mac was running Mac OS 9
directly. The program will present its own menu bar
and windows like any application, but its graphic
style will be that of Mac OS 9 rather than Mac OS X.
(Also, applications running under Classic won't
take advantage of OS X's advanced features such
as protected memory – for more details of these,
see "How Mac OS X Works" on page 215.)

If you've used Mac OS 9, you'll know that it has its
own version of the Finder, with the same role as in
Mac OS X – helping you arrange and move folders
and files. There is only one Finder used across the
whole of Mac OS X and Classic, though: the
standard Mac OS X Finder. This is a key difference
between running Classic and running Mac OS 9
natively: in Classic, you can still see the Mac OS X
Desktop, Dock and any open windows underneath.

When Classic starts up
within Mac OS X, you
can see the old Mac
OS 9 startup window
as the second operating
system loads.

Quick tip

Some of your Classic applications may need access to the Internet to function fully. The easiest way to provide this connection is to open your connection in Mac OS X in the usual way, then switch to the application in Classic.

You can click on any of these elements to carry on working in Mac OS X as usual and will see the Mac OS X menu bar restored at the top of the screen. In effect, you have two operating systems running in parallel, each controlling its own applications. The appropriate OS takes over depending on which program you're running, but with Mac OS X always controlling what's going on.

Controlling Classic

To start using Classic, open System Preferences and click Classic. The Classic area has two tabs to look through. The Start/Stop tab enables you to start running Classic, but you must first choose a Mac OS 9 System Folder for Classic to use. If you followed our advanced installation procedure in the chapter "Installing Mac OS X", you'll see two possible options here: choose the System Folder that's on the same hard disk partition as your Mac OS X System folder.

If you use Classic often, you can tick the checkbox "Start up Classic on login to this computer". This means that Classic is ready to run applications immediately you start your Mac, rather than

Photoshop Elements is just one of the thousands of existing Mac OS applications you can use in Mac OS X with the Classic tool.

making you wait as it loads after you first run a Classic application. This option applies only to your Login and doesn't affect those of other users.

You can also shut down Classic in three different ways: a controlled shutdown that first saves any unsaved documents you were working on; a controlled restart that saves documents and starts Classic from scratch; and a Force Quit that is unable to save any changed documents. Use this last option only when a Classic application is badly misbehaving.

The Advanced tab is largely for people who are used to working in Mac OS 9 and know some of its more advanced tricks. The Startup Options pull-down menu enables you to load the Extension Manager on startup, which enables you to choose which Extensions are loaded. You can also start up with no Extensions running, or choose a particular keyboard combination to hold down as you start: you can press down up to five keys and it then restarts Classic using the keys that you've pressed down. It's hard to see exactly why you'd need this, though, because all the options you'd need (rebuild Desktop, restart without Extensions) are catered for

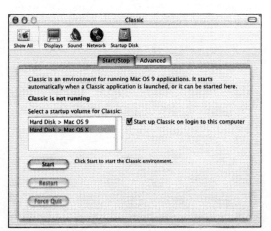

Use the Classic area in System Preferences to decide which Mac OS 9 System Folder you should use to power Classic.

already... You can also set a period after which Classic goes to sleep if you haven't been using it, which frees up processor and memory resources for Mac OS X. You can also rebuild the Desktop, but since you can't actually see the Classic Desktop, this is more of a troubleshooting measure.

Classic basics

During its startup process and while it's active, Classic behaves in almost exactly the same way as Mac OS 9 running independently. Like Mac OS X itself, Classic relies on its own System Folder, which holds the core operating system software it needs to function. The System Folder also contains any Extensions that some hardware devices may need to run, such as drivers.

As we've seen, a Classic application uses the old-style menu bar, which performs essentially the same role as the Mac OS X menu bar but is set up in a slightly different way:

Apple menu
While Mac OS X's Apple menu lists options that change the state of the entire operating system, the Classic Apple menu is more a store of tools you may need to call upon at any time – almost like the Dock in Mac OS X. The Control Panels option is the Classic equivalent of System Preferences, giving

Use the Startup Disk area in System Preferences to select the operating system your Mac should load the next time it starts up.

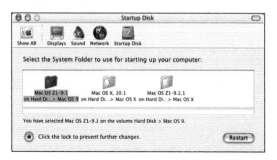

you access to detailed settings. You can also access small applications like a calculator and the Chooser, which helps you select printers and network access.

Application-specific menus

Next to the Apple menu sit several further menus, all specific to the application that's running at that moment. Many of the most common menu names to appear are the same as the ones often seen in Mac OS X applications, such as File and Edit, and have broadly the same roles. One important distinction is that the Quit option is found in the File menu under Classic.

Menu bar clock

As in Mac OS X, there's a clock in the menu bar. Click on it once to briefly see the date.

Application menu

Placed on the far right of the menu bar, the Classic Application menu has a different job from the Mac OS X menu of the same name, although both always show the name of the front application. This menu lists all active Classic applications as well as the Finder and other programs running in Mac OS X. Choose any name from the menu to switch to that program.

Running Mac OS 9

From time to time, you may want to operate your Mac in Mac OS 9, rather than in Mac OS X or a combination of Mac OS X and Classic. Perhaps you own a hardware device that lacks the software driver necessary to work in Mac OS X; or there's a program that doesn't function correctly under Classic. You may also want to configure some elements within your Classic setup, and it's easier to do this while running under the System Folder that Classic uses.

To switch from Mac OS X to Mac OS 9, open System Preferences and click Startup Disk. This lists any System Folders on your Mac that it's able to run – usually after a brief check of the hard disk to make sure they're still in place. Click on the System Folder you wish to start under, and you'll see a message confirming your selection. You can then click the Restart button to switch OS.

It's similarly easy to switch back to Mac OS X from inside Mac OS 9. Go to the Apple menu and select **Control Panels > Startup Disk** to see a list of available operating systems, listed according to the hard disk volumes on your Mac. It should be simple to locate the Mac OS X System folder; click on its icon to highlight your selection, then press the Restart button in the Startup Disk window.

You can see some familiar Mac OS X elements when you run Mac OS 9: the System Folder and Library are clearly visible on your hard disk. It's crucial that you don't move files in these folders while in Mac OS 9, or you might find yourself unable to start Mac OS X. You can also access the Users folder and your Home folder, so you can open documents in both Mac OS X and Mac OS 9 if you have the correct applications.

If you have Mac OS 9.1 or later alongside Mac OS X on your Mac, you can use its Startup Disk Control Panel to switch into Mac OS X.

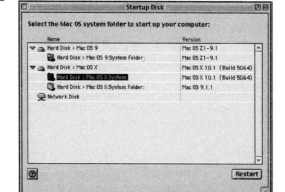

The final Mac OS X folder present is Applications, and it's worth taking a look in here. Many of the applications inside show a plain, generic icon and now end with the filename extension **.app**: these programs work only in Mac OS X. If you see an application with a coloured icon, however, you can use it in Mac OS 9 as well as X. You might want to make Aliases of any compatible applications and move these into your "Applications (Mac OS 9)" folder as a reminder that these programs are available to you under OS 9.

24 Just My Type

Fonts are essential to making any text in Mac OS X
look good, whether it's words in a document or
options presented in the menu bar. Every piece of
text, whether on-screen or printed out, uses a font to
define the shape of its characters; an able designer
can use fonts to transform a plain document into an
object of beauty. Strictly speaking, a font is a specific
typeface in a particular size and style: Times and
Helvetica are well-known typeface families; Times
Italic is a typeface; and Times Italic 12 point is a
font. The terms are often confused, though, and
commonly used interchangeably.

Mac OS X includes a
selection of high-quality
fonts to make your
documents suitable
for any occasion.

Installing fonts

Mac OS X includes an excellent selection of fonts
that are ready to use after the OS is installed; you
can also buy more and install them yourself. Fonts
can be located in five different areas on your Mac;
Mac OS X will collate all of these and show them in
one list. You should decide where to install a font
based on who is likely to need it and what kind of
licence the font was sold with. Don't make fonts
with a single-user licence available over a network,
for example.

Library/Fonts
Any user on your Mac can access fonts stored here.
Only users with Administrator privileges can add
or remove fonts in this folder.

~/Library/Fonts
You are the only person to have access to fonts
stored in this location within your Home. When
other users log in, even if they have the access
rights to use the same applications, they won't be
able to use these fonts. It's just as if someone sent
you a document created on another computer
using fonts not installed on yours: provided you
have an application capable of opening that type of
file, you'll be able to read the text, but only using
substitute fonts.

System/Library/Fonts
Any user on your Mac can access fonts stored here.
However, Mac OS X uses these fonts in elements
like the menu bar, so no user is allowed to add or
remove fonts in this folder.

Network/Library/Fonts
If your Mac is functioning as a network server,
others on the network can access fonts stored here.
Similarly, you can access fonts held in the Network
volumes of other Macs available over the network.

Quick tip

If you are running an
application in Classic,
it can access only the
fonts held in its own
System Folder; none
of the fonts in other
locations is available.

System Folder/Fonts

The System Folder is used by the Classic environment to run applications written for versions of the Mac OS before OS X. Once the folder is selected for Classic use in System Preferences, you can use these fonts in both Mac OS X or Classic.

Working with fonts

Many applications enable you to choose a font to use in a document, while some enable you to choose fonts used in the application windows and dialogue boxes as well. You can also typically change various aspects of your chosen font in a document, such as its size, colour or text styling (bold, italics, etc.). Some applications simply present a long list of fonts as an option in the menu bar; move your mouse pointer down the list to select the font you want. Others (including TextEdit) use Mac OS X's built-in Font panel, which presents similar basic options but also offers tools to help manage your font collection as it grows.

When you first open the Font panel, you can see a list of installed fonts in one column, with two further columns to its right. Click on a font to see the different styles available for that font in the next column, and use the end column to select a size for the font in your document.

Extend the Font panel to see a column of differently-themed font collections, helping you choose a font more quickly. You can add further collections.

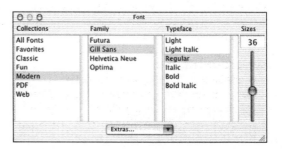

If you use the panel's resizing control to make the panel wider, another column appears on the far left. This lists your "collections", which group together fonts of a similar kind to make it easier to select the font you need. Collections don't actually have any further functions – you can't activate or deactivate particular groups of fonts, for instance, as you can with certain commercial utilities such as Suitcase – but they are an aid to housekeeping and ease of selection. There are a few collections already; click on one to see the fonts belonging to that collection.

In the Extras pull-down menu is an option to edit your collections. Use the columns in the editing window to add fonts to a collection or remove them, or click the **+** button in the corner to add a new collection. Click the **–** button to delete any collection; this doesn't actually delete any of the fonts listed, just the particular grouping in which they're listed.

Quick tip

Select "Edit Sizes" from the Extras pull-down menu to change the standard font sizes listed in the Font panel. You can also choose to have a slider control displayed for the most minute degree of control.

Key Caps

Some fonts are "pictographic", which means they include only patterns and symbols instead of standard alphanumeric characters (letters and numbers). It's a real test of memory to recall which key on your keyboard triggers which symbol in a pictographic font like Zapf Dingbats, but you can use the Key Caps application (stored in **Applications/Utilities**) to look up the symbol you need. Key Caps presents an on-screen representation of your keyboard; select the font you're using from the Font menu so you can see

Use the Key Caps application when you're not sure how to get a certain character in the font you're using, like the Zapf Dingbats pictographic font shown here.

Quick tip

Apple plans to offer a facility to buy and download fonts over the Internet. You can check on its progress by selecting "Get Fonts" from the Extras pull-down menu, which connects you to Apple's online font store.

which keys produce which symbols. Hold down modifier keys like Shift to see the additional symbols you can type by holding down that key.

Key Caps also helps you look up key combinations to generate the accents used in some characters, such as the acute accent used in French. If you hold down the Option key while in Key Caps, you can see some keys with heavy borders around them and accents shown on the keys. To type the accent you want, hold down Option and press the relevant key for the accent you want, then release the keys and type the character over which you want the accent to appear. For example, you can type Option-E then E to produce the French é, or Option-U then O to get the German character ö.

25 How Mac OS X Works

To finish our tour of Mac OS X, this chapter looks briefly at some of the technologies that enable Mac OS X to offer the massive lineup of features and tools we've explored. You don't need to know how the operating system works to use it, but we hope you enjoy discovering the power underneath the elegant user interface.

The power of Unix

At the very heart of Mac OS X is the operating system Unix, perhaps the most robust and powerful OS available today. The secret of Unix's success is that its core components are free – no-one has to pay a penny to obtain them and install them. Unix is the most treasured asset of the open-source software movement, people around the world who believe in sharing knowledge and experience for the good of all. The idea of open-source is that a piece of software programming code is made freely available, so that any programmer with enough skill can adapt it and improve on it – on the condition that they in turn make their changes freely available too. As the cycle continues, you end up with a worldwide community of programmers who may never meet, but share ideas and suggestions to make the software in question as good as it can get. It's decades of work like this that has made Unix so formidable.

Many companies and other groups, such as university-funded projects, have taken the Unix core and constructed a broader operating system on top, supplying users with a graphical interface and developers with the tools to build programs to run on these more complete OSs. The best-known example before Mac OS X was Linux, a rich interpretation of Unix developed by Norwegian Linus Torvalds and offered to the world for free. Linux has attracted a great deal of interest from many people over the last few years. Less of a household name, but with equally appreciative support, is X-Windows, which provides an alternative user interface for the Unix core. In its first year, though, Mac OS X has already become the world's most popular Unix variation – even if many of the people using it have never heard of Unix.

Apple has of course adhered to the Unix tradition by giving some of its knowledge back to the community. Darwin is a completely free, open-source implementation of the core of Mac OS X, although it is missing OS X's graphical interface

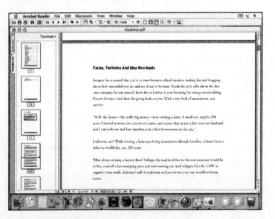

Adobe used the Carbon development environment to bring its application Acrobat Reader to Mac OS X. The choice means that the same application also works in Mac OS 9.

and many other Apple technologies, so it's not
aimed at your average computer users.

Core advantages

OS X is the first version of the Mac OS to be based
on Unix, and it is fundamentally different from
previous versions of the Mac operating system.
(That's why it requires Mac OS 9 also installed on
your Mac to generate the Classic environment to
run pre-OS-X software.) Why this fundamental
change? In a nutshell, in order to implement certain
features that Apple decided were vital in a modern
operating system for the 21st century.

These vital features include protected memory
and pre-emptive multitasking, which are both
invaluable when a computer is performing several
tasks at once. As users expect more from their
computers, and software becomes more complex
and demanding, computers aren't simply
performing one task after another in a straightforward sequential way. Graphic designers, for
example, might want a 3D scene to continue to
render at the same time as they turn to some other
task; or you might simply want to be able to type
a letter while your computer is printing another
document or downloading a file from the Net. At
any given time, you might have several programs
active, and multiple processes might be running
simultaneously, as a quick look at Mac OS X's
Process Viewer can demonstrate.

Though it was capable of some degree of "multi-
threading" – so that you could continue working
while files were being copied in the Finder, for
example – the traditional Mac OS had reached its
limits in handling such complexities. The Unix core
of Mac OS X handles them much better, and thus
ensures greater stability and efficiency. Because
critical functions run in "protected" memory space,

the operating system itself is unlikely to crash even if some other process should encounter a problem. Because OS X can allocate processor time between processes according to their importance rather than just as they demand it (that is, it can multi-task pre-emptively, rather than just co-operatively), the whole system operates more efficiently.

In the same way, Mac OS X incorporates other advanced features, such as support for the latest networking technologies; symmetric multi-processing, which makes far more efficient use of computers with more than one processor in them; and improved memory management, which uses hard disk space as "virtual memory" so cleverly that applications should never run short of the memory they need to work in (and you never have to allocate an application more RAM manually, as you had to do in previous versions of the Mac OS). In all these ways, Mac OS X is geared up for the demands of users and their software into the future.

Power tools

Slotting into Mac OS X's Unix kernel is a series of other technologies, each with a specific job to do.

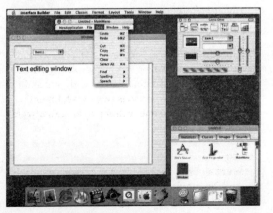

Included with the boxed version of Mac OS X, the Developer Tools CD provides software and tutorials to help you create your own Mac OS X application.

For example, Apple's QuickTime system handles video and audio playback, while OpenGL is a powerful technology that handles 3D graphics and animation. Why are these technologies separate from the core operating system, rather than built into it? The reason for this "modular" structure is that these technologies are standards not restricted to the Mac; they exist for other operating systems as well, and are widely supported by software developers and device manufacturers.

The graphics acceleration subsystems built into your Mac, for example, can work automatically with OpenGL to enhance your games and 3D design work – and so can the graphics cards in computers running other operating systems. Game designers supporting OpenGL can be confident that a wide variety of computers will be able to reproduce the effects they add to their games.

Apple has said that it chose the best technologies around to handle specific tasks within Mac OS X – OpenGL for 3D display; QuickTime for media playback; a system called "Quartz", based on Adobe's PDF format, for 2D graphics, which builds in support for transparency, font smoothing, and other clever techniques for improved display.

Application frameworks

With the Unix core and supporting technologies in place, what's needed next is a framework in which your Mac OS X applications can be designed and programmed. Apple provides two development environments for anyone wanting to write software for Mac OS X:

Carbon
There are an estimated 10,000 applications available for the Mac, a massive investment on the part of thousands of individual programmers and the

hundreds of software publishers they work for. While the Classic environment can run most of these, we obviously want to use our favourite programs directly in Mac OS X and take advantage of the new OS's advanced features.

Apple has provided a development environment specifically to serve that need. Carbon is designed to help developers convert their existing Mac applications to work fully within Mac OS X with the minimum effort on their part. The process might still take months, because programs have to be thoroughly tested to make sure they work smoothly (and because some aspects of OS X require quite a bit of work to implement, such as the new system it uses to attach dialogue boxes to the window they pertain to, instead of just popping up and preventing you doing anything further until you attend to them); but it's far easier than starting from scratch. An added bonus is that developers can choose to make their "Carbonised" application still run in some older versions of the Mac OS.

Cocoa

There are many programmers who have never created any software for the Mac, preferring to cater for users of other computer platforms instead. Cocoa is a second development environment for those writing for the Mac for the first time, or simply choosing to build an existing application from scratch. It's actually derived from an existing set of programming tools for the now-defunct operating system NextStep, elements of which have been incorporated into Mac OS X. An added benefit of this approach is that many former NextStep developers have become some of Mac OS X's most enthusiastic advocates, enjoying the twin bonus of a much larger possible audience for their products and programming tools that let them convert their existing NextStep applications quite easily.

Mac upgraders

One of the interface changes introduced by Mac OS X is the idea that dialogue boxes, such as Open and Save dialogues, appear in the form of "sheets" that are attached to the window they relate to, so you can turn to another task if you wish before attending to them. This is more logical in a multi-tasking system than the old "modal" dialogues, which prevented you doing anything else until you attended to them. However, not all OS X applications implement sheets, so you may find the behaviour of dialogue boxes varying from application to application.

Developer tools

If you bought the boxed edition of Mac OS X, you should have a Developer Tools CD with a grey label. This contains applications and extensive documentation for anyone wanting to write software for Mac OS X. Programming is an intensely technical vocation and shouldn't be approached lightly, but this CD is a great place to start, and Apple is distributing it to make it easy for more developers to write for OS X. Tools include Project Builder, which helps you quickly set up a basic framework for your application, and Interface Builder, which enables you to construct windows, menus and palettes in minutes.

(There are of course other tools around for creating applications, including packages such as REALbasic and MetroWerks' CodeWarrior, which is designed for experienced professional software authors.)

Quick tip

For more information about REALbasic, visit REAL's Website, **www.realsoftware .com**. For more on CodeWarrior, see **www .codewarrior.com**.

Hey, good-looking

Finally, there's the user interface that enables you to manipulate all these elements. The interface is the combination of menus, windows and other controls that you use continually in Mac OS X. Mac OS X's interface, which Apple has named "Aqua", is the most sophisticated ever devised, with lush photographic icons and sophisticated typography enhancing a huge array of tools for every level of expertise. Indeed, so important is the interface – the part of the OS with which you actually deal, day by day – that to many people the interface *is* the operating system. In this chapter, we've explored a little of what goes on under the surface, but if you can master the tools and functions that the user interface puts at your disposal, you can honestly say that you've got to grips with Mac OS X.

And that's not all...

For future updates and corrections to this book, plus the opportunity to add your own feedback and ongoing discussion, visit

www.macunlimited.com
the online Mac magazine
news reviews features tutorials

Plus, for all your Internet needs, whether you want to set up your own site, graduate to a custom database or e-commerce, or just get connected...

www.macunlimited.net
mac dedicated service provider
dialup hosting co-location streaming